FILIALITY: THE HUMAN SOURCE

-volume one-

Composed, Compiled and
Translated into English by
Dharma Realm Buddhist University
Buddhist Text Translation Society
Talmage, California ~ 1983

FILIALITY: THE HUMAN SOURCE, Volume One

Verses and selections composed, translated, and compiled by:
                        Bhikshuni Heng Ch'ih, Ph.D. and
                        Bhikshuni Heng Tao, Ph.D.
Edited by: Upasika Susan Rounds Ph.D. and Bhikshuni Heng Ming
Certified by: Venerable Abbot Hua and Bhikshu Heng Tso
Stories on Filial Piety Translated by: Upasika Terri
                        Nicholson
            Reviewed by: Bhikshuni Heng Tao, Ph.D.
            Edited by: Bhikshu Heng Tso and
                        Bhikshuni Heng Ch'ih, Ph.D.
            Certified by: Venerable Abbot Hua and
                        Bhikshuni Heng Tao, Ph.D.

Printed in the United States of America
First Printing: July 1983
ISBN #: 0-88139-006-2

Proofing: Bhikshuni Heng Chü, Bhikshuni Heng Ming,
              Bhikshuni Heng Cheng, Upasika Terri Nicholson,
              and Sari Epstein
Typing: Bhikshuni Heng Ch'ih, Ph.D. and Bhikshuni Heng Liang
Photographs: Upasaka Kuo Kuei Nicholson
Graphics and Layout: Bhikshuni Heng Liang
Original drawing, page 102: Sarah Owen

For information and Booksales:

Gold Mountain Monastery   Gold Wheel Monastery
1731 15th Street   1728 West 6th Street
San Francisco, CA 94103   Los Angeles, CA 90017
Tel. (415) 626-4204   Tel. (213) 483-7497
      (415) 861-9672

            City of Ten Thousand Buddhas
            P.O. Box 217
            Talmage, CA 95481
            Tel. (707) 462-0939

Namo Shakyamuni Buddha

Buddhist Text Translation Society
Eight Regulations

A translator must free himself or herself from the motives of personal fame and reputation.

A translator must cultivate an attitude free from arrogance and conceit.

A translator must refrain from aggrandizing himself or herself and denigrating others.

A translator must not establish himself or herself as the standard of correctness and suppress the work of others with his or her faultfinding.

A translator must take the Buddha-mind as his or her own mind.

A translator must use the wisdom of the Selective Dharma Eye to determine true principles.

A translator must request the Elder Virtuous Ones of the ten directions to certify his or her translations.

A translator must endeavor to propagate the teachings by printing sutras, shastra texts, and vinaya texts when the translations are certified as being correct.

- Namo Bodhisattva Who Regards the Sounds of the World -

TABLE OF CONTENTS

THE GREATEST GOOD

The greatest good is to be filial.
The greatest evil is to rebel against
   one's parents, teachers, and elders.
Among the myriad conducts, filiality is
   number one.
It stems from the heavenly nature,
   inherent in us all,
And is perfected through sincere acts
   of body, mouth, and mind.

FIELD OF BLESSINGS

Virtue begins with filial practices toward
    our parents.
Our parents are like the sun and moon,
And like heaven and earth.
They are living fields of blessings
In which we can plant the seeds of goodness
And see that they bear a bounteous harvest.

REPAYING KINDNESS

Even the raven returns to the nest
    to feed its aging mother.
The young lamb kneels to drink
    his mother's milk.
If we people fail to repay our parents'
    kindness,
Then we don't even measure up to
    the conduct of these animals.

LAMENT

The tree would be still,
      but the wind does not stop.
The child wishes to be filial,
      but his parents are gone.

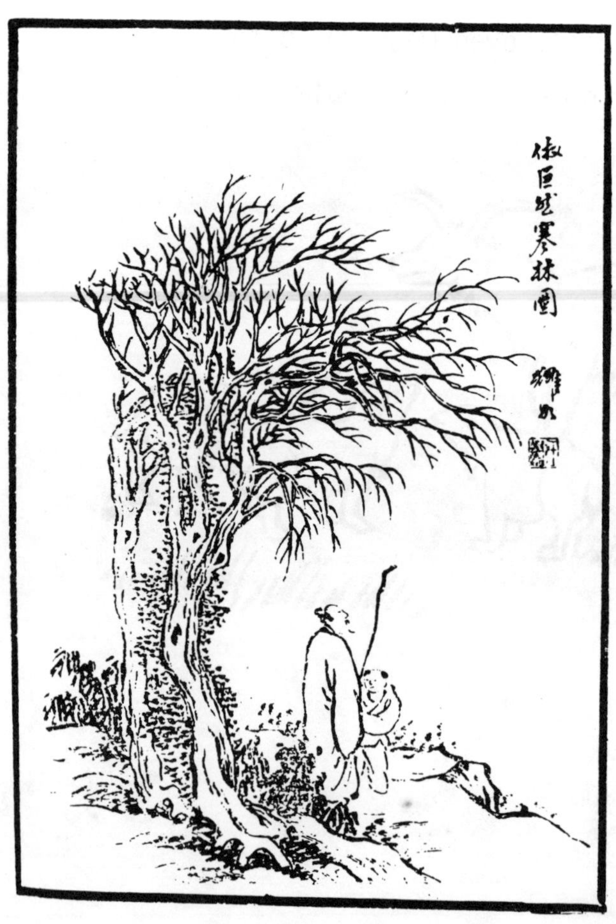

FAMILIES

Families that amass good deeds

Will certainly enjoy great fortune.

Families that only do evil,

Will certainly attract calamities.

             —excerpt from the I CHING,
                         The Book Of Changes.

WHY DOES DISCORD ARISE?

The reason there are wars and strife,
Quarrels in families,
Divorces, separations, and unhappy children,
Is because people have forgotten their roots
And neglected to be filial.
If we "nurture the origin and solidify
   the roots,"
Then families will be harmonious,
People will get along,
And the world will not be plagued
   with fighting.

WHEN I SERVE MY PARENTS

When I serve my parents in filiality,
I vow that living beings
Will serve the Buddhas skillfully,
And protect and nourish everything.

When you are being filial to your parents, you should also vow that all living beings serve the Buddhas skillfully, and be filial to the Buddhas. When there is no Buddha dwelling in the world, you should be filial to your parents. Your parents are living Buddhas at home. Because our parents gave us our physical bodies, we should be filial to them and repay their kindness. As it is said:

Their kindness is vast like the heavens,
without limit.
We should exhaust our bodies in toil
for our parents.

Just consider how your mother carried you in her womb for nine months. Cardinal Yü Pin has told us all that he is against abortion. Many people support the act of abortion in this day and age. That is not a benevolent attitude. It doesn't matter whether people are young or old, or whether they have old-fashioned ideas or modern ideas, no one should support abortion. That is because it does not accord with the nature of human beings. Cardinal Yü Pin said, "Abortion is like killing the sprouts of the human species." He is right. Babies are just like sprouts of the human species. Abortion is killing those human sprouts. I really agree with him.

If you are filial to your parents, you should also be filial to the Buddhas. In fact, protecting and supporting the Buddhadharma is the same as being filial to your parents. When you're filial to your parents, that is the same as being filial to the Buddhas. Therefore, between the Buddhas and your parents there should be no distinction. If a person is filial to his parents, the Buddhas will be happy. They will surely praise the filial child saying, "Good indeed! Good indeed!"

-excerpt from FLOWER ADORNMENT
SUTRA, Pure Conduct, Chapter 11
Commentary by Master Hua

SERVING A GOOD TEACHER

"Good man, in seeking a Good Knowing Advisor, you should not grow weary. In seeking a Good Knowing Advisor, do not give rise to a sense of satiation or boredom. In inquiring from a Good Knowing Advisor, do not shirk from toil and suffering. In drawing close to a Good Knowing Advisor, do not harbor thoughts of retreat. In making offerings to a Good Knowing Advisor, do not rest. In receiving the teachings of a Good Knowing Advisor, do not invert his teachings. In studying a Good Knowing Advisor's principles, do not give rise to doubts. In hearing a Good Knowing Advisor explain the doors of escape, do not be hesitant. In seeing a Good Knowing Advisor accord with activities of afflictions, do not criticize or complain. Toward a Good Knowing Advisor, produce a mind of deep faith and veneration, without changing..."

-excerpt from ENTERING THE DHARMA REALM
Part VII

A GOOD KNOWING ADVISOR

"Good man, the Good Knowing Advisor is like a kind mother, in that he gives rise to the Buddha's seed. He is like a kind father, in that he vastly benefits. He is like a nurse, in that he protects one and stops one from doing evil. He is like a teacher, in that he shows one what a Bodhisattva should study. He is like a good guide, in that he can open up the path of paramitas. He is like a skilled physician, in that he can heal the sickness of afflictions. He is like a snow mountain, in that he makes grow the medicine of all-wisdom. He is like a valiant general, in that he banishes all terror. He is like a ferryman, in that he enables one to get out of the torrents of birth and death. He is like a boat captain, in that he can cause one to arrive at the Jeweled Continent of Wisdom. Good man, you should, with proper mindfulness, reflect upon all Good Knowing Advisors in this way."

-excerpt from ENTERING THE DHARMA REALM
Part VII

BRIGHT LIGHT

Moreover the Bodhisattva emits a bright
light which has a pure flavor able to cast out
the poisons in all food and drink. From constantly
making offerings to the Buddhas, to the Sangha,
and to one's parents, one comes to accomplish this.

-excerpt from FLOWER ADORNMENT SUTRA
"Worthy Leader," Chapter 12

WARNING TO STEPPARENTS

-by Great Master Lien Ch'ih
of the Ming dynasty

There are people who treat their blood-offspring with the utmost tenderness and care, cherishing them as if they were their own eyes. However, they look upon their stepchildren as mere weeds and brambles, and recklessly whip and humiliate them. They feed their own children nutritious and savory foods, yet they feed their stepchildren nothing but coarse food, or worse, just let them starve. They dress their own children in silk and satin, providing them the warmest clothes, and yet they give their stepchildren tattered clothes which can't even ward off the bitter cold.

But those children happen to be the offspring of their own spouses. How can anyone be so biased and unfair to a child who belongs to his or her own spouse? Heaven will frown on people like that. The ghosts and spirits will glare at them with displeasure. In future lives these people are most unlikely to be blessed with children, and even if they do become parents, their own children will suffer accidents and harm. How can we fail to heed these words of caution!

HOW CAN WE REPAY SUCH KINDNESS?

Our parents are our origin.
It is they who bore and raised us,
Giving us this human body.
If we do not seek to repay this debt of kindness,
We can't even be called human.
How can we repay their kindness?
By cultivating a compliant and loyal attitude,
And by being principled, public-spirited
   and just,
So we can grow up to be morally responsible
   adults.

BENEFITTING ANCESTORS

When one child attains the Way,
Nine generations of ancestors are reborn
in the heavens.

———————

Heaven and earth take filiality as the
highest virtue.
If one child is filial, the whole family
is peaceful.
Filial children in turn give birth to
filial children,
And all the filial ones will become
bright sages.

THE BUDDHA SPEAKS THE ULLAMBANA SUTRA

Na Mo Homage to the Ullambana Assembly of Buddhas and Bodhisattvas. (*Recite three times*)

Thus I have heard, at one time, the Buddha dwelt at Shravasti in the Garden of the Benefactor of Orphans and the Solitary. Mahamaudgalyayana had just obtained the six penetrations and wished to cross over his father and mother to repay their kindness for raising him. Thus, using his Way Eye, he regarded the world and saw that his deceased mother had been born among the hungry ghosts. Having neither food nor drink, she was but skin and bones. Mahamaudgalyayana felt deep pity and sadness, filled a bowl with food, and went to provide for his mother. She got the bowl, screened it with her left hand, and with her right hand made a fist of food. But before it entered her mouth, it turned into burning coals which could not be eaten. Mahamaudgalyayana called out and wept sorrowfully, and hastened to return to the Buddha to set forth all of this.

The Buddha said, "Your mother's offenses are deep and firmly rooted. You alone do not have enough power. Although your filial sounds move heaven and earth, the heaven spirits, the earth spirits, twisted demons, and those outside the way, Brahmans, and the Four Heavenly King Gods are also without sufficient strength. The awesome spiritual power of the assembled Sangha of the ten directions is necessary for liberation to be attained. I shall now speak a Dharma of rescue which causes all those in difficulty to leave worry and suffering, and to eradicate obstacles from offenses."

The Buddha told Maudgalyayana, "The fifteenth day of the seventh month is the Pravarana Day for the assembled Sangha of the ten directions. For the sake of fathers and mothers of seven generations past, as well as for fathers and mothers of the present who are in distress, you should prepare an offering of clean basins full of hundreds of flavors and the five fruits, and other offerings of incense, oil, lamps, candles, beds, and bedding, all the best of the world, to the greatly virtuous assembled Sangha of the ten directions.

"On that day, all the holy assembly, whether in the mountains practicing dhyana samadhi, or obtaining the four fruits of the Way, or walking

beneath trees, or using the independence of the
six penetrations to teach and transform Sound
Hearers and Those Enlightened to Conditions, or
provisionally manifesting as Bhikshus when in fact
they are Great Bodhisattvas on the Tenth Ground--
all complete with pure precepts and ocean-like
virtue of the holy Way--should gather in a great
assembly and all of like mind receive the Pravarana
food.

"If one thus makes offerings to these Pravarana Sanghans, one's present father and mother, parents of seven generations past, as well as the six
kinds of close relatives will escape from the three
paths of suffering, and at that time attain release.
Their clothing and food will spontaneously appear.
If the parents are still alive, they will have
wealth and blessings for a hundred years. Parents
of seven generations past will be born in the heavens. Transformationally born, they will indepen-
dently enter the celestial flower light, and experience limitless bliss."

At that time the Buddha commanded the assembled
Sangha of the ten directions to recite mantras and
vows for the sake of the donor's family, for

parents of seven generations. After practicing
dhyana concentration, the Sangha accepted the food.
When they first received the basin, they placed
it before the Buddha in the Stupa. When the assembled Sangha had finished the mantras and vows
they received the food.

At that time the Bhikshu Maudgalyayana and the
assembly of Great Bodhisattvas were all extremely
delighted and the sorrowful sound of Maudgalyayana's
crying ceased. At that time Maudgalyayana's mother
obtained liberation from one kalpa of suffering
as a hungry ghost. Maudgalyayana addressed the
Buddha and said, "This disciple's parents have
received the power of the merit and virtue of the
Triple Jewel, because of the awesome spiritual
power of the assembled Sangha. If in the future
the Buddha's disciples practice filiality by offering up the Ullambana basins, will they be able
to cross over their present fathers and mothers
as well as those of seven generations past?"

The Buddha replied, "Good indeed! I am happy
you asked that question. I just wanted to speak
about that and now you have also asked about it.
Good man, if Bhikshus, Bhikshunis, kings, crown

princes, great ministers, great officials, cabinet
members, the hundred ministers,   and the tens of
thousands of citizens wish to practice compassionate
filial conduct, for the sake of the parents who
bore them, as well as for the sake of fathers and
mothers of seven lives past, on the fifteenth day
of the seventh month, the day of the Buddha's Delight, the day of the Sangha's Pravarana, they all
should place hundreds of flavors of foods in the
Ullambana basins, and offer them to the Pravarana
Sangha of the ten directions. They should vow to
cause the length of their present fathers' and
mothers' lives to reach a hundred years without
illnesses, without sufferings, afflictions, or
worries, and also vow to cause seven generations
of fathers and mothers to leave the sufferings of
the hungry ghosts, to be born among humans and
gods, and to have blessings and bliss without limit.

The Buddha told all the good men and good
women, "Those disciples of the Buddha who cultivate
filial conduct should in thought after thought,
constantly recall their present fathers and mothers
when making offerings, as well as the fathers and
mothers of seven lives past, and for their sakes

perform the offering of the Ullambana basin to the Buddha and the Sangha and thus repay the loving kindness of the parents who raised and nourished them."

At that time the Bhikshu Maudgalyayana and the four-fold assembly of disciples, hearing what the Buddha said, practiced it with delight.

End of the Buddha Speaks the Ullambana Sutra

TRUE WORDS FOR REPAYING PARENTS' KINDNESS

NA MWO MI LI DWO

DWO PWO YE

SWO HE.

(Recite over and over.)

(After reciting the Sutra, the assembly recites the mantra while circumambulating the Buddha.)

NATURALLY GOOD

People at their birth are by nature good.

Their natures are close to the Way,

But their habits take them away from it.

If there is laxness in teaching them,

Their natures will change.

The proper way to teach

Is to be single-minded.

—excerpt from the THREE CHARACTER
CLASSIC

21

THE BUDDHA SPEAKS THE SUTRA ON CAUSE AND EFFECT IN THE THREE PERIODS OF TIME

Translated by Bhikshuni Heng Tao
Reviewed by Bhikshuni Heng Ch'ih
Edited by Upasaka David Rounds
Certified by Venerable Abbot Hua
and Bhikshuni Heng Ch'ih

At that time, Ananda was on Magic Mountain, together with twelve hundred fifty in the assembly. Ananda made obeisance with his palms together, circumambulated the Buddha three times, and knelt with his palms joined. Then he asked Shakyamuni Buddha this question: "During the Dharma-Ending Age, all the living beings in Southern Jambudvipa will give rise to much unwholesome karma. They will not revere the Triple Jewel, or respect their parents. They will be lacking in the Three Bonds.[1] The Five Constants[2] that safeguard the universal obligations between people will be in disharmony and disarray. Beings will be poor, destitute, lowly, and vile. Their six faculties will suffer impairment. All day long they will engage in killing and harming. Moreover, they will not be of equal status; some will be wealthy

---

[1] The "Three Bonds" refers to the relationship between ruler and minister, between father and son, and between husband and wife.

[2] The Five Constants are humaneness, righteousness, propriety, wisdom, and trustworthiness.

while others will be poor. What are the conditions leading to these various different rewards
and retributions? We disciples pray that the World
Honored One will compassionately explain each
one of these for us."

The Buddha told Ananda and the assembly of
great disciples, "You should now listen attentive-
ly. Good indeed, good indeed! I will clearly
set forth all of this for you. All men and women
of the world, whether they be poor and lowly or
wealthy and noble, whether they be undergoing
limitless sufferings or enjoying blessings without
end, are all undergoing the rewards or retributions
which are due to causes and effects from their
past lives. What should they do from now on?

"First, they should be filial and respectful
to their parents. Next, they should reverently
believe in the Triple Jewel. Third, they should
refrain from killing and instead liberate the living. Fourth, they should eat pure vegetarian food
and practice giving. These acts will enable them
to plant seeds in the field of blessings for their
future lives."

Then the Buddha spoke these verses on cause
and effect:

Wealth and dignity come from one's destiny
From causes planted in lives in the past.
People who hold to this simple principle
Will reap good fortune in lives in the future.
Kind men and women, listen to the causes,
Hear and remember this Sutra's reminder
Of the causes and effects of karmic deeds
In the past, in the future, and in the present.
Cause and effect is no small care,
True are my words; don't take them lightly.
Why are some people officials at present?
Because with gold they gilded the Buddhas
In their past lives, long long ago.
It's from their practice in lives in the past
That they reap in this life a rich fruition.
The purple gown and golden cordon--
The honored marks of higher office:
Should you seek them, seek with the Buddhas.
Gilding the Buddhas is your own gain;
Robing Thus Come Ones, you robe yourself.
Don't say it's easy to become an official;
It cannot happen if causes aren't planted.

What are the causes of owning a carriage
And riding on palanquins? People like that
Were builders and menders of bridges and roads.

Why are some people wearers of satin?
That is because in times in the past,
Robes they gave as gifts to the Sangha.

Sometimes people have plentiful goods,
The reason, in fact, again is quite fair.
In the past those people gave food to the poor.

Others don't have food or drink,
Who can guess the reason why?
Before those people were plagued with a fault:
Stingy greed made them squeeze every penny.

The well-to-do among us dwell
In very tall mansions and vast estates.
The reason is they gladly gave rice,
Lavishing gifts of grain on monasteries.

Enjoying blessings and justly prosperous,
Are people who reap a fitting reward.
In times now past they helped build temples
And saw that the Sangha had huts and shelters.

Some people's features are fine and perfect.
Surely the reason for such rewards
Is that beautiful flowers they offered to
    Buddhas.

Why are some people gifted and wise?
In former lives they ate pure food
And remembered the Buddhas with mindful regard.

Look at men whose wives are loyal,
Their reward comes now for what happened before:
Their conditions are strong in the Buddha's door.

Some have marriages lasting and meaningful.
Their happiness doesn't happen by chance.
The cause this time is the hanging of canopies
And streamers before the Buddhas' statues.

Some happy fellows' fathers and mothers
Enjoy long lifespans, contentment, and ease.
Where is the source for rewards such as these?
They protected orphans in times now past
And regarded all elderly ones as their own.

Orphans must live without fathers and mothers
Since before they shot down birds for sport.

How does one get lots of children and grand-
    children?
By letting birds fly from their cages to
    freedom.

In raising children, some really fail badly.
It's because before they drowned female infants.

When barren, people won't bear any children.
That's their due for committing promiscuous
    deeds.

Some have long lifespans, why are they lucky?
Liberating creatures, they ransomed lives.

Have you seen how many suffer short lifespans?
Their wanton slaughter of beings is why.

Lonely are men whom no women will marry.
They're paying their debt for committing adultery.

Widows bear a sad retribution.
They held their past lives' husbands in scorn.

Servants and slaves made that bondage themselves
By neglecting repayment of goodnesses done them.

Bright are the eyes of some fortunate beings.
Before Buddhas they offered lamps filled with oil.

The blind of this world bear a heavy burden
For past failure to tell the way clearly to
     travellers.

Some people's mouths are very misshapen.
They blew out lamps on the Buddhas' altars.

To be deaf and mute is a dreary existence.
Reward appropriate for scolding one's parents.

How do people get to be hunchbacks?
They berated and laughed at those bowing to
     Buddhas.

Take heed of malformed hands, my friend.
They betray people prone to evil.

Fellows with crippled and useless feet
Ambushed and robbed with reckless abandon.

Most cows and horses were humans before--
People who didn't settle their debts.

Many former people are now pigs or dogs
Because they injured and cheated others.

Illness and pain: an effect inevitable
For bestowing meat and wine on the Buddhas.

Freedom from illness: a fine reward
For relieving the sick by bestowing medicines.

The fate of imprisonment catches some people
Due to fiendish deeds and a failure to yield.

Death by starvation: due retribution
For stopping up holes of rats and snakes.

Appropriate that a victim of poisoning
Caused aquatic poisoning; dammed up waters.

Abandoned, forlorn,   rejected beings
Were cruel of old, abusing others.

The stature of some is extremely short.
Before, they read Sutras spread out on the floor.

Vomiting blood? Believe it's from first
Eating meat, then reciting the Sutras.

Another deed that determines deafness:
To not listen well to Sutra recitals.

Sores and scabies bother some people
Who gave stinking fish and flesh to the Buddhas.

People who reek with a terrible stench
Sold inferior scents and phony goods.

Why do some by their own hand hang themselves?
Before, they used nooses to capture their prey.

All those widowed, alone, unwed, or orphaned,
Are now paid justly for former jealousy.

Those struck by lightning, consumed by fire,
Rigged their scales to better their business
    income.

Fierce tigers and snakes that feast on people
Are enemies bearing resentments from lives before.

In our myriad deeds, whatever we do,
We reap our own rewards, it's true.

Who can we blame for our woe in the hells?
Who can there be to blame but ourselves?

Don't say that cause and effect is unseen.
Look at you, your offspring, heirs, and grand-
    children.
If you doubt the good of pure eating and giving,
Look around and find those enjoying fortune.
Having practiced of old, they now harvest
    abundance.

To cultivate now will bring blessings anew.
Those who slander the cause and effect in this
    Sutra
Will fall and have no chance to be human.

Those who recite and uphold this Sutra
Are supported by Buddhas and Bodhisattvas.

Write out this Sutra, study it hard
And in the future your families will flourish.
Uphold this Sutra atop your heads
To avert disasters and fatal accidents.

To lecture this Sutra on Cause and Effect
Is to sharpen your wits in successive rebirths.

Chanting this Sutra on Cause and Effect
Will make one revered, well-regarded by all.

Print and distribute this precious Sutra
And reap rebirth as a ruler or king.

To verify former cause and effect,
Regard Mahakashyapa's golden body.
A case of future cause and effect:
Bhikshu Good Star slandered the Dharma
And lost his chance for human life.

If cause and effect contained no truth,

Why did Maudgalyayana seek to rescue his

   mother

From the hells to save her from suffering?

Those who trust the words of this Sutra as true,

Will all be reborn in the Western Land of Bliss.

To speak of present cause and effect

To proclaim future and past as well,

Is a deed that could never be done to its end.

Join at the door of the Triple Gem.

With blessings and wholesome belief one can enter

The door, supported by gods and dragons,

Dragons and gods who won't let you down.

For every part of giving you practice,

You'll reap ten thousand parts reward.

Such blessings are stored in a solid treasury,

For enjoyment in future rebirths without end.

If you care to know of past live's causes,

Look at rewards you are reaping today.

If you wish to find out about future lives,

You need but notice what you're doing right now.

END OF THE BUDDHA SPEAKS
THE SUTRA ON CAUSE AND EFFECT
IN THE THREE PERIODS OF TIME

EMPEROR YU SHUN, WHO MOVED HEAVEN
WITH HIS FILIAL VIRTUE

Yu Shun lived in the Shang dynasty. When he
was very small his mother died and his father
soon married again. When his second wife gave birth
to another son, he named the child Hsiang. Even
though Yu Shun was an exceptionally good child,
his stepmother favored her own son and was often
very harsh with Shun. His little brother took
advantage of the situation and every time something
went wrong in the household, he made it look like
Shun was responsible for the mishap. Unfortunately
Shun's father did not recognize what was happening.
In fact, the people around him called him Gu Sou,
meaning that he was blind to what was going on
right under his nose. He couldn't tell right from
wrong.

Because Shun's father couldn't tell the true
from the false, he always believed the lies that
his wife and Hsiang told him about Shun. He would
beat Shun as punishment for things which he hadn't
even done just because they acccused him of them.
Even so, Shun continued to be obedient and kind
to his parents and loving and protective of his

little brother. Although he was so filial to his parents, he still could not win their hearts.

Finally, over a very small matter, his stepmother threw him out of the house. With no home to go to, Shun went to live in the forest where he ate wild nuts and fruits. He saw a family of birds in a nest and their closeness made him feel sad

and ashamed. He thought to himself, "If I use all
my effort to make a living, maybe my parents and
brother won't look down on me anymore." So he
went to the village and helped people plow their
fields. Because he was so kind and well-mannered,
the people were fond of him and taught him how to
farm. As he grew older, he went back to the forest and marshes to make a living. The animals
in the forest protected Shun and helped him in
his work. The wild elephants came to help him
plow the fields and the birds sowed the seeds,
dropping them one by one into the soft earth.
Everything that he grew, all the rice and vegetables, he sent home to his parents to show them
his respect.

Shun became a legend in his own time and soon
even the Emperor heard about him. In Zhung Kuo,
people believed that the Heavens chose the Emperor,
and because of that, they trusted his goodness and
wisdom. It so happened that Emperor Yau was getting old and had been thinking for some time of
finding someone to inherit his position. But
he knew that the person he chose would need to be
virtuous enough to rule the people justly and with
kindness. When it became obvious that the people
loved and respected Yu Shun, Emperor Yau decided

to test him to find out if he was truly one of
great virtue.

When people do not have true virtue, power
and money will cause them to be selfish and arro-
gant. Therefore, Emperor Yau gave Shun one of
his daughters to be his wife and provided them
with a house to live in and a herd of cows and
sheep. He then watched to see how Shun handled
his gifts.

Meanwhile, when Shun's family heard that he
had become the Emperor's son-in-law, they were
overcome with jealousy. Shun's younger brother
Hsiang was especially covetous of his elder
brother. Hsiang influenced his father against
Shun to the point that the two of them became
determined to keep Yu Shun from inheriting the
throne. So hard did their hearts grow that they
even devised schemes to murder him!

One day Hsiang went to Shun and said, "Father
wants you to come and fix the roof of the storehouse."

Of course Shun said, "I'll come right away."
When he arrived at his father's house, Hsiang helped him carry the ladder to the storehouse. But
as soon as Shun climbed up on the roof and began
fixing the shingles, Hsiang carried that ladder

away.   Then he returned to the storehouse, set it on fire, and hid away to watch the "future Emperor" go up in flames. Fortunately the Heavens were moved by Shun's virtue and a strong wind arose out of nowhere. It began to blow the fire mysteriously to one side of the roof, allowing Shun to get to the unburned side and jump off.

His brother ran home, feeling a bit frightened by what he had just witnessed, and told his mother, "Mother! When I set fire to the storehouse, a strange wind came and kept the fire from getting near Shun. So he is still alive!"

However, his stepmother was still blinded by her jealousy. She convinced her husband to go once again and entice Shun into another trap. Her "Gu Sou" husband agreed. "Son," he said to Shun the next day, "I don't know who was so careless yesterday. I'm really sorry. Thank goodness you didn't get hurt! Can you come over tomorrow and dig the well a bit deeper? We can't get any more water from it."

Of course Shun agreed immediately to honor his father's request. Arriving the next morning as promised, Shun was a little more cautious. Even though he would never have harbored the thought that his little brother was intent upon

murder, he was wise enough to take some precau-
tions. "Let's get some rope, Father. I'll tie
one end around my waist and give the other end
to you two. When I pull on the rope, it means
that I'm ready to be pulled up. All right?" His
father and brother agreed, so Shun collected some
tools, tied the rope around his waist, and slowly
climbed down into the well. When he got to the
bottom, it was cold, wet, and dark, but he paid
no attention to the discomfort. He simply set
about the task his father had asked him to do and
began digging. He dug for a long time before he
finally reached water. When he was ready, he
pulled on the rope attached to his waist to signal
his father and brother. When nothing happened in
response, he groped around in the dark and discovered that the entire rope was there at the
bottom of the well with him. His father and brother had thrown it in after him, trapping him at
the bottom of that dark, cold tomb.

He yelled for help until his voice gave out
and then stopped and collected his thoughts. He
would just have to try to find a way out by himself. Basically the walls of a well are slimy
and slippery and so vertical that it's impossible

to climb out from bottom to top. The bottom of
a well is full of water, so there's really no
way out, unless you can fly like a bird. But since
there was nothing else to do, Shun groped about
in the pitch dark hoping for the impossible.
Strange as it may seem, just as he was about to
give up all hope, he came upon an opening in the
side of the well which led into a cave. Without
a moment's hesitation, Shun crawled into the
hole. He seemed to have extra strength in his arms
and legs, for somehow he was able to grip the
slippery, wet rocks and make his way forward through
the hole. Crawling and climbing like that for a
long time, he finally came to the end of the cave-
like passage and found the mouth, leading out into
sunshine. For the second time, his father and
brother had been unable to kill him.

Since Shun escaped both these dangerous
situations without harm, his parents and brother
didn't dare devise any more plots to kill him. And
because Shun continued as always to be good to
his family, their cold hearts began to melt slowly
and they eventually felt quite ashamed of all the
horrible things they had done to him because of
their jealousy. Gradually their attitude toward
Shun changed.

The Emperor, of course, heard every detail of Shun's life from his daughter. Seeing how Shun had won the hearts of the people all around him, how great his virtue was, and how he had even been able to influence his parents to change their evil ways, Emperor Yau was virtually convinced that Shun was capable and worthy of governing the country in any situation. However, just to be sure he decided to give Shun one more test.

It hadn't rained in three months and so the Emperor asked Shun to seek the compassion of the rain and thunder spirits on his behalf. After receiving these instructions, Shun returned home and told his wife what the Emperor had asked of him. In order to accomplish this task, Shun had to first go deep into the marshes and find the Thunder Spirit. His wife told him he should go quickly and gave him a small florescent pearl which she said would be of valuable use to him.

After searching for a long time, Shun fin-ally found the footprints of the Thunder Spirit and knew that he was nearby. Calling out, he said, "Honored One, my humble name is Shun and I have come representing the Emperor to seek your compassion. There has been no rain in three months and the earth and its plants are thirsty

for water. Please use your power to make it rain."
Suddenly the marshes grew very dark and Shun saw
great bolts of lightning and heard the tremendous
roar of thunder. As he bowed to thank the Thunder
Spirit, rain began to fall in torrents. Now it
was so dark that he couldn't see to find his way
out of the marshes. But still Shun was not afraid.
All he felt was happiness that the earth would
have water to drink. Then suddenly he remembered
the pearl his wife had given him. When he took
it out, it glowed so brightly that he found his
way out without any trouble. When he returned
safely, the Emperor was smiling. Now he was sure
that he had found someone with enough virtue to
rule the country. He knew that the people would
be safe and happy with Yu Shun as their Emperor.

REAP AS YOU SOW

The Buddha told Kashyapa, "Living beings who vex and bother their parents, causing their minds to become nettled and afflicted, will reap the retribution of having many illnesses.

"Those who make offerings to their parents as well as to sick people will reap the reward of having very little illness.

"Those who do not cherish or respect their parents or the sages will command very little awesome strength. Those who delight in serving their parents and the sages will attain great awesome power."

-excerpt from

THE SUTRA OF

DIFFERENT

KARMIC

RETRIBUTIONS

A FILIAL DAUGHTER

Limitless aeons ago a Buddha named Pure Lotus Eyes appeared in the world. His lifespan was forty aeons. During the period after his passing, an Arhat who had great merit and who crossed over living beings, teaching them as he met them, encountered a woman named Bright Eyes who made an offering of food to him.

"What is your wish?" asked the Arhat.

Bright Eyes replied, "On the day of my mother's death I performed good deeds to help rescue her, but I do not yet know in what path she has been born."

Out of pity for her, the Arhat entered into samadhi to contemplate. He saw that Bright Eye's mother had fallen into an evil path where she was undergoing extremely great suffering. The Arhat asked, "When your mother was alive, what deeds did she do that she now has to be undergoing such great punishment in an evil path?"

Bright Eyes replied, "My mother liked to eat fish, turtles, and other seafood. She especially like to eat fish eggs and by doing so, she killed millions of lives. Oh Venerable Compassionate One, how can she be saved?"

The Arhat pitied her and offered her this expedient method. "With a sincere mind, be mindful
of Pure Lotus Eyes Buddha and make carved and paint-
ed images of him to benefit the living and the dead."

Hearing his advise, Bright Eyes renounced
everything she loved and used it for the drawing
of an image of that Buddha and in order to make
offerings to his image. She wept sorrowfully as
she gazed respectfully at the Buddha. Suddenly,
in the late hours of the night, as if in a dream,
she saw the Buddha's body, dazzling gold in color
and as large as Mount Sumeru, emitting great light.
The Buddha said to Bright Eyes, "Before long your
mother will be born in your own household and as
soon as she can know hunger and thirst, she will
be able to speak."

Shortly after that, a maidservant in the house
bore a son who spoke before he was three days old.
Lowering his head and weeping sorrowfully, he
said, "In life and death, one must undergo retributions for one's own deeds. I am your mother and
have long been in darkness. Since leaving you I
have constantly been reborn in the great hells.
As a result of receiving the power of your good

deeds, I have been able to be reborn, but only as
a poor son in a low-class family. My lifespan,
moreover, will be short. After thirteen years, I
must fall into the evil paths again. Do you have
some way to help free me from this suffering?"

When Bright Eyes heard the child's words,
she knew without a doubt that he was her mother
and, choked with sobs, she said to the child,
"Since you are my mother, you should know your
own past offenses. What deeds did you do that
caused you to fall into the evil paths?"

The servant's child said, "I have to undergo
these retributions because I killed and slandered.
If I had not received the merit which you earned
for me, I still would not be free of that bitter
suffering, because my karma would be such that
I could not yet have gotten free."

On hearing this, Bright Eyes asked, "What
happens during retributions in the hells?"

The servant's son answered, "It is unbearable
even to speak of those sufferings, but even if I
could describe them, it would take hundreds of
thousands of aeons to tell you."

When Bright Eyes heard this, she wept bitterly

and said into empty space, "May my mother be for-
ever free of the hells, and after these thirteen
years may she be released from her heavy offenses
and leave the evil paths. O Buddhas of the ten
directions, have compassion and pity me! Hear the
far-reaching vows which I am making for the sake
of my mother. If she can leave the bad paths for-
ever, leave the lower classes, leave the body of
a woman, and never again have to endure these sufferings, then, before the image of the Buddha Pure
Lotus Eyes, I vow that from this day on, throughout
hundreds of thousands of millions of aeons, I
will rescue living beings who are suffering in the
hells for their offenses or who are caught in the
other evil paths. I will rescue them all and cause
them to leave the realms of the hells, the hungry
ghosts, the animals, and so forth. Only when the
beings who are suffering for their offenses have
all become Buddhas will I myself become a Buddha."

After making this vow, Bright Eyes clearly
heard the Buddha Pure Lotus Eyes say to her,
"Bright Eyes, you have great compassion to be able
to make such a great vow for your mother's sake.
I see that your mother will cast off this body

after thirteen years and will be born a Brahman
with a lifespan of one hundred years. After that
life she will be born with a lifespan of aeons
in the Land of No Concern, after which she will
accomplish Buddhahood and cross over as many people
and gods as there are sand grains in the Ganges."

Shakyamuni Buddha, who was relating this
true story, told Samadhi Self-Existent King, "The
Arhat with great merit who helped Bright Eyes
is now Inexhaustible Intention Bodhisattva. The
mother of Bright Eyes is Liberation Bodhisattva.
Bright Eyes herself is now Earth Store Bodhisattva.

-Excerpt from the EARTH STORE
BODHISATTVA SUTRA

REPAYING PARENTS' KINDNESS

-Contemporary Filial Piety

-Papa Joe

-Nature's First Law

-Leaving the Home Life:
    The Highest Form of Filial Piety

CONTEMPORARY FILIAL PIETY

Sherry and Kenton Hyatt drove out from Cambria to bring the monks (Bhikshus Heng Sure and Heng Ch'au whose bowing pilgrimage took them up the coast of California, bowing once every three steps and dedicating the merit to repay the kindness of their parents and teachers, as well as for peace and tranquility for the world) some hot food. With them in their orange VW bus was "half of Cambria" said Kenton. In all there were seven: Abraham and Rosebud, age two and two months respectively, Sherry's father, Papa Joe Miller, age eighty-six, and Lynne Borges and her baby daughter Elizabeth.

"I was so happy to read that Buddhists don't cut their ties with family," said Sherry.

The meal was set out on a cliff above the Pacific but a rain squall moved us back into the bus. Papa Joe who is ailing with the problems of old age, is "not able to walk well on some days." He was originally going to stay in the car and miss the picnic; when the rain came we gathered the party around him.

"You bow in this weather, don't you?" asked Sherry.

"Rain or shine," replied Heng Ch'au.

Sherry: "That's the other thing about you that impressed me right away. You're not out for the easy path, I believe."

Heng Ch'au: "You're the first person to say that right out. People say to us 'take it easy!' and I answer, 'No, we take it hard.' You realize Heng Sure is not being impolite. He's made a vow of silence."

Sherry: (laughter) "Yes, we know. I can really see the advantages of silence. All the trouble you save! I talk all the time without thinking so I stick my foot in my mouth--left and right."

Kenton: "Can you tell me briefly what Buddhism is all about in your view?"

Heng Ch'au: "The Buddhadharma is a method to break your false thoughts and your attachments, so that you can respond to the world as it is right now. I came to it because it gets right to the heart of what's important in life. Buddhism is about ending birth and death and helping other people."

Kenton: "How do you do that?"

Heng Ch'au: "Right now we're doing it in just one of the many ways possible. We're bowing so as to end disasters and calamities, to turn back the suffering and bad vibes that fill the world. Buddhism holds that all suffering comes from the presence of the self. We're not bowing to anything in particular. But we are trying to bow away our egos--our selfishness and self-centered ideas."

Sherry: "That's what people see in your work."

Heng Ch'au: "I think so. People aren't really interested in two individuals--it's what we represent. Are you working for others? That's what counts."

Kenton: "How come Buddhists are identified with seclusion?"

Heng Ch'au: "Basically monks and nuns are mendicants--wanderers. Temples and monasteries are to them like base camps are to mountain climbers. We leave our homes and the whole universe becomes a home."

Sherry: "So you don't have to go to a temple to be a practicing Buddhist?"

Heng Ch'au: "If you really practice, then the

whole world is a temple. Buddhadharma transcends all boundaries. It doesn't get stuck in any distinctions. That's what we like about it. It's really democratic."

Kenton: "Hmm. Buddhism might be the first true workingman's religion. I'm a tour guide at Hearst Castle. Can I be a Buddhist and a tour guide,too?"

Heng Ch'au: "Look at it this way, Kenton. All the tour guides at Hearst Castle are Buddhists. Only some don't recognize the fact yet. Start with that principle. It's only a matter of time." (laughter).

Kenton: "How did you two find your way to Buddhism?"

Heng Ch'au: "Like everyone else, we looked hard for something that had heart, something that lasted. As I said, I wanted to do what was important. To me that meant repaying the kindness of my parents and doing good for others. I couldn't bear the thought of my life just going down the tube."

Kenton: "Well sure, that's everyone's dream. No one plans for this life to be a waste, but somehow it happens to a lot of people."

Heng Ch'au: "We had to put down a lot to find the Dharma. We took a lot of false roads along the way. You have to come a long way to find out that you had what you wanted all along."

Kenton: "Do you take days off from the bowing?"

Heng Ch'au: "Our rest is in our work and our work is restful. We like what we do so we do it all the time."

Kenton: "Very few people in the world can say that."

Heng Ch'au: It's said that we are 'born drunk and die in a dream.'"

Sherry: "Wow! I like that. Ain't it the truth!"

Heng Ch'au: "We have a dream of success or fame or all pleasures or desires satisfied and then when we get what we desired, it turns out to be more suffering. If you want a lot of money, you have to hire people to guard it from thieves. If you eat a lot, you get overweight. If you buy a lot of clothes, you can't wear them all--what a lot of hassle."

Sherry: "This comes from false thoughts and

attachments in your view, right?"

Heng Ch'au: "Precisely."

Sherry: "Well, you two have so little. Seems like it would be hard not to always think about getting more."

Heng Ch'au: "We've learned that what we need, we get, if we are sincere. What we don't need, we don't get."

Sherry: "For instance, if you take this wilderness route you're talking about, you'll need a jeep, won't you?"

Heng Ch'au: "See? There's a false thought. If we need a jeep, by the time we reach the turn-off a jeep will appear."

Sherry: "Oh, so the 'what if' questions are false thoughts?"

Heng Ch'au: "Right. The point in cultivation is to be here and now. When you're worried about a jeep in the future, you're no longer here and now. You're then, already."

Sherry: (laughter) "I get it."

Heng Ch'au: "So, when then comes you've already been there. Then when the jeep doesn't show up, you get all afflicted and suffering begins.

The best way to be is like little Abraham here.
Tomorrow's his second birthday, right?"

"Right."

"Well, you know he doesn't spend two seconds
today thinking about his party. But then when it
comes, he's right there totally into it, same as
he is right now."

Sherry: "Children are really pure. When you
shave your heads that way, it makes you look like
kids again in a certain way."

Heng Ch'au: "Exactly. It's another way to
return to your original face. The point is not
to decorate the body or cover it with vanity and
phoniness."

Kenton: "How do you begin being a Buddhist?"

Heng Ch'au: "You could say we're all Buddhists
to begin with, but we wandered away from our original home. We all begin cultivating by holding
the five precepts--the rules of living. They are:
no killing, no stealing, no sexual misconduct,
no lying, and no intoxicants, drugs, or cigarettes.

Sherry: "Boy, that really says it, doesn't
it!"

Heng Ch'au: "When you hold the precepts

then the whole world is a pure place, a temple.
You can hold them anywhere. The point of precepts
is right here, to stay pure to open the road to
concentration and wisdom.

Sherry: "Sounds right on."

Heng Ch'au: "Abraham isn't clouded over by
sex and confusion. He doesn't tell lies. But
we've all learned these habits, we've all gotten
covered over."

All: "Amen."

Heng Ch'au: "Precepts give you the purity
back. They allow you to drop the covers. When you
hold precepts, pretty soon you can say 'see what
I had before I got dirty?'

"The Bodhisattva does not seek nobility...
    he does not seek riches or benefit...
    he only cares about upholding pure
    precepts.
                    -excerpt from FLOWER ADORNMENT SUTRA,
                     "Ten Practices Chapter"

"To be human you must first of all be
    aware that your father's and mother's
    kindness towards you is higher than
    heaven and deeper than the ocean. If
    you don't consider repaying it, you

57

should be truly and greatly ashamed. Such
a one is unfit to be called a person."

-excerpt from WATER-MIRROR REFLECTING HEAVEN
by Venerable Master Hsuan Hua

Kenton: "We had a chance to invite Papa Joe
to live with us and so we could look after him. We
just didn't believe that a rest home was necessary.
After the decision was made, sure enough, we found
room. A big house in Cambria came our way and I
found a good job in this area that we like, and
jobs are incredibly tight around here."

Sherry: "Things are really going well since
we got all our family back together again. I can't
tell you how many blessings have come to us because
of taking care of my father."

Kenton: "We were down and out in Santa Ana,
California. I had just come out of college, had
all my plans made, and was looking ahead. I was
going to be a teacher just when the job market did
not want any teachers. It was a hard lesson."

Sherry: "Then my father's health got bad and
we didn't believe in rest homes. We thought,
what's the most natural, most simple way to put
all the pieces of our lives together? We decided

to start by giving my father the treatment he deserves. Let's bring Papa Joe home where he belongs. And this is the neat alternative to rest homes. We thought, we can do it, so we just did it."

Heng Ch'au: "Boy, that's great. The path to sagehood starts right here with filial piety. Wonderful. You know why Abraham respects you and is such a happy child? Because he sees how you treat Papa Joe. If you respect your parents, you will win your children's respect."

-recorded by Bhikshu Heng Sure,
ONE HEART BOWING TO THE CITY
OF TEN THOUSAND BUDDHAS, V.6.

PAPA JOE

What is mindfulness of parents' kindness? Alas! My parents! They bore me with hard labor, ten months in the womb, three years at the breast, drying my bottom, changing my diapers, swallowing bitterness and feeding me sweetness. Only then was I able to become a person.

- excerpt from "Essay on the Exhortation to Bring
forth the Great Bodhi Mind" by Great Master
Hsing An (d. 1735 A.D.)

The Hyatts, a young family from Cambria, drove

out on a blustery day to share a meal offering.
There was Ken and Sherry, their two small children,
Abe and Rose, still in diapers. And all bundled up
in blankets, warm and dry, sitting in the back seat,
was their aging father, Papa Joe.

Papa Joe could no longer walk. He showed signs
of senility and required a lot of care and patience.
But the Hyatts didn't seem to be put out or burden-
ed. Ken carried Papa Joe out to the picnic spot
and when a rainstorm came up, he quickly wrapped
him in a blanket and carried him to the car.

We all squeezed together in their V.W. bus
along with a friend of theirs and her infant, making
nine in all. They listened with bowed heads as
Heng Sure and I chanted the meal offering and rang
the hand bell. Over hot vegetable soup and home-
made bread, the Hyatts told their story.

"Papa Joe was ready for the nursing home,
but we didn't feel right about it, so we asked
him to please come and live with us. We felt he'd
be doing us a favor. We were so happy when he
agreed."

"At the time," said Ken, "we had no house,
no money, and I couldn't find work. But you know

right after our decision to ask Papa Joe to come
and live with us, things opened up. A big old
house came our way and I got a fine job offering
in this area even, where jobs are almost non-exist-
ent."

Papa Joe sits quietly, smiling now and again,
as the kids crawl around his legs chasing a ball.
He's so obviously happy and at peace.

"We feel all our blessings came from doing
right by Papa Joe," says Mrs. Hyatt. "We just did
what came naturally."

A cold rain blows against the windows. The
Hyatts say they came out because they felt somehow
Buddhism stood for filiality and just doing the
right and natural things in life. The Hyatts
are drawn to the moral precepts of Buddhism and
the spiritual goal of "going back to the root,
returning to the source." It's as if the principles
of Buddhism are already deeply rooted in their
minds, in a timeless natural understanding. They
identify with the Buddhadharma as much or even more
so than with their home state, Ohio. (Someone men-
tions that the monks are from the midwest and that
Heng Sure is from Ohio. Papa Joe perks up and grins,

reaching out to shake hands. "Ohio! That's where I'm from." Papa Joe has been listening to every word about Buddhism, nodding when he agrees. When he hears "Ohio" something connects and suddenly Buddhism is very close to home, like it was as American as corn and apple pie).

"But what really excited us was when we heard that filiality is a fundamental teaching in Buddhism We just had to come out," says Mrs. Hyatt.

The ultimate expression of filiality is cultivating the Way. To repay the kindness of parents is a primary motivating factor in spiritual history. It is a belief shared by the ancients and enlightened teachers of all countries over the centuries. The Buddha, Shakyamuni, spoke the *EARTH STORE BODHISATTVA SUTRA* for the sake of his mother and also set forth the Bodhisattva precepts in the *BRAHMA NET SUTRA* to repay his parents.

> At that time, Shakyamuni Buddha first
> sat beneath the Bodhi tree, after realiz-
> ing the supreme enlightenment, he set
> forth the Bodhisattva precepts out of
> filial compliance towards his parents,

his masters among the Sangha, and the
Triple Jewel. Filial compliance is
a Dharma of the ultimate Way. Filiality
is called precepts, and is also called
restraint and stopping.

Why the precepts? Because precepts are the
only way one can end the suffering of birth and
death and leave the turning wheel of the six paths.
Filiality is an ultimate teaching moreover, because
one who is enlightened sees all living beings as
his own parents. Therefore, he restrains himself
to act with utmost kindness and compassion and
filial regard toward all that lives.

All male beings have been a father to
me in past lives and all females have
been my mother. There is not a single
being who has not given birth to me
during my previous lives, hence all
beings of the six destinites are my
parents.

It is from this understanding of the oneness
of all beings and the inter-relatedness of all

things that Buddhism takes it roots. The Hyatts
recognized it immediately. Filiality is basic to
being a person and to accomplishing ultimate wisdom.

> If you want to be a person, the very
> first thing you should know is that
> compared to the sea, your parents'
> kindness is deeper; compared to the
> sky, your parents' kindness is higher...
> If you plan to repay them, you must
> first learn to have virtue and to
> teach living beings to cultivate the
> Way. It is said, 'If one child obtains
> the Way, nine generations will leap over
> birth and death.'

-excerpt from WATER-MIRROR REFLECTING HEAVEN,
by Venerable Abbot Hsüan Hua
Entire entry excerpted from ONE HEART BOWING, V.6, Bhikshu
Heng Ch'au

NATURE'S FIRST LAW

There are four rules inseparable in

obtaining happiness and prosperity

in your next life. The first of these

is to be dutiful to parents.

-excerpt from THE SUTRA OF CAUSE AND EFFECT

The Buddha teaches filiality as Nature's
First Law. The Buddha speaks truth, with principles
older than time itself. Old age is a natural badge
of honor. But in the younger generation, being
old is often viewed as a crime.

Can you imagine us years from today,

Sharing our park bench quietly?

How terribly strange to be seventy.

- Simon and Garfunkel

Until this century, old people lived among
their kin. Big families held together. Youth
honored and respected the wisdom and experience
of elders. Divorces were few, runaway children
fewer yet, suicides and alcoholism rare. The family
absorbed the stress and confusion of life. People
lucky enough to have their seniors alive enjoyed
happiness, blessings, and a sense of belonging
sadly lacking in the contemporary, alienated world.

But all creatures fear death and prefer the dream of immortality. Science and materialism give people new solutions to the riddle of impermanence for the first time in history. "No deposit, no return"; throw away the old, hide grandparents in the seniors' home. We replace anything that wears out, including old people. We toss out jobs, mates, hearts, and kidneys as easily as changing T.V. channels.

Filiality is forgotten in a graceless scramble for eternal youth. Growing old in the twentieth century is an unpardonable sin. "Everyone for himself," has become a universal disease. We perserve the Ego and repair its failing, leaking, body-shell. We ignore the signs everywhere shouting "Wake up! A tree that cuts its roots cannot stand long."

Buddhists face aging and death with an even mind. Nature's cycles revolve in perfect harmony. Who would feel complete in a year without winter?

For everything there is a season and a time for every purpose under heaven: a time to be born, and a time to die...

—excerpt from THE HOLY BIBLE, Ecclesiastes Ch. 3v, 1-9

It's time we restored the dignity of old age,
time to rescue our elders from solitary confinement
at the seniors' home. Filiality is Nature's First
Law.

—excerpt from ONE HEART BOWING, V. 6, Heng Sure

LEAVING THE HOME LIFE:
THE HIGHEST FORM OF FILIAL PIETY

The Hyatt family brought Heng Ch'au and me a fresh appreciation of the value of leaving the home-life. Papa Joe Miller, ailing and infirm, was a happy man. His son-in-law and daughter and their two children shared a special joy in life. And we in turn, rejoice in their upholding the dharma of filiality. Filiality is a natural blessing. Respect for elders is right in the heart.

If so, why have we chosen to cultivate the Way instead of staying at home and honoring our parents? Because ancient wisdom teaches:

> When one child obtains the Way,
>
> Nine generations of ancestors
>
> are reborn in the heavens.

Our families gave us solid ground for growing up into world citizens. We feel extremely lucky to have good parents. Only because of their deep kindness were we able to step up to the challenge of life as Buddhist disciples. Cultivators of the Way forsake personal security and transfer their filial duties to a bigger responsibility: they devote their lives not to maintaining one family line but to preserving the supreme path to liberation for all beings.

-excerpt from ONE HEART BOWING, V.6, Bhikshu
Heng Sure

THE STORY OF FILIAL SON WANG

At a place where there are true cultivators,
demons often come to test them. They come to test
the cultivators, to see if their hearts are true.
One such example that comes to mind is that of
Filial Son Wang. This is an event that happened
during the Ch'ing Dynasty in the village of Ch'ang
Ch'un in Manchuria:

Filial Son Wang, whose given name was Meng
Hsing, sat by his mother's grave to observe the
practice of filial piety. The practice is an ex-
cellent method of cultivating the Way. Filial Son
Wang was so strict in his ascetic practices that
he ate only raw food. Every day people would come
to the grave to offer him rice, and every day he
would eat just a handful of raw rice grains. It
is the case that if a person truly cultivates, then
others will come and make offerings to him, so a
lot of people offered Filial Son Wang rice and
money. But he wasn't the least bit greedy; he
didn't want the money. He'd just let it lay on
the ground. The copper coins would pile up in
huge stacks, while the paper bills would just get
blown away by the wind. But he didn't pay heed
to any of it. He had truly seen through it all
and put it all down.

One day, some bandits came along. Seeing the
large stacks of coins on the ground, they scooped
them all up and stole off with them. Filial Son
Wang didn't even bat an eye. When the bandits
finished counting the money, they found that it

was a considerable sum, and they had this thought,
"If there's this much money outside the grave,
surely he must have even more stashed away inside.
Why don't we go again and rob him clean this time?"
So during the night they went to the grave where
Filial Son Wang was sitting. The head bandit
placed a sharp knife right against Wang's neck
and threatened him, saying, "Bring out all your
cash--it's your money or your life!"

Filial Son Wang told him, "You already took
away all the money this morning."

The bandit wouldn't believe him. He persisted
with his threat. "If you don't bring it out, I'll
knife you!"

Filial Son Wang said, "Even if you kill me,
I can't give you any money, because you already
took it all."

The bandit still didn't believe Filial Son
Wang, and so he jammed the knife into the latter's
neck, making a cut two to three inches deep. He
slashed Wang's throat. Then the bandits disappeared into the night. Filial Son Wang continued
to sit upright. Though his throat was slashed,
his breath was not completely cut off.

In the morning, the people discovered the
stabbing and reported it to the authorities. Because Filial Son Wang was so respected, the authorities turned out in full force. Ambassadors from
America, England, Japan, and France all came along
with the Chinese officials. They said to Wang,
"We're determined to find the thief who knifed you
and to avenge the wrong done you. There are five

nationalities that reside in the village of Ch'ang
Ch'un. Since you can't talk, we'll each ask you
in turn. If the murderer happens to be the same
nationality as the person who asks you, just nod
your head."

And so they took turns in asking him--the
American, the Englishman, the Frenchman, the Japanese, and the Chinese. But each time Filial Son
Wang shook his head, "no". They were perplexed!
"Well, if the murderer doesn't belong to any of
these five nationalities represented here, could
it be the case that heaven is responsible?"

At that, Filial Son nodded his head firmly,
and shortly after that he died. Since that was
the way Filial Son Wang interpreted the incident,
the authorities couldn't press any charges, so
they buried him in a mound alongside his parents'
graves.

Nothing happened for several decades, and
everybody thought that the case of Filial Son Wang
was over and done with. Then came a time when the
Japanese, who were occupying Manchuria, decided to
renovate the village of Ch'ang Ch'un. In order to
rebuild the town, they first set about excavating
the graves. All the graves were dug up. But when
the workers tried to excavate Filial Son Wang's
grave, they'd faint right on the spot before they
could dig even a shovelful. They would just keel
over and fall to the ground with a thud. The people were amazed and perplexed. This happened
repeatedly, until eventually they reported this
to the Japanese foreman, who personally came to

try his hand at digging. On the first shovel, he
also rolled over unconscious. But the Japanese
weren't going to let that stop them. They tried
to use dynamite to blow up the grave. But the
dynamite wouldn't go off. Next, they dropped bombs
from airplanes overhead, but each time the bombs
landed, they wouldn't go off. Then a voice came
out from the grave; it said in a clear sound,
"It's not yet time to move my mother's bones;
whether my grave gets moved or not is up to heav-
en's will."

People understood, and nobody tried to meddle
further with his grave. In Manchuria, the grave
of Filial Son Wang is one of the most famous land-
marks. Everyone in the entire province knows about
it.

Now you think about it: Filial Son Wang was
such a good cultivator, eating only a handful of
raw grains every day, and yet he was assassinated.
Was it the case that the Dharma Protecting Spirits
didn't come to protect him? No, they were just
testing him to see if he really had a mind for the
Way, whether he was willing to sacrifice his body
for the Dharma. Therefore, although his body was
killed, his spirit continues to live on, and his
name continues to inspire the generations for
posterity.

At the City of Ten Thousand Buddhas, demonic
obstacles are an everyday occurrence. Why? It is
because we are true. Many people from the outside
slander the City of Ten Thousand Buddhas and try
to create all sorts of trouble for us. But is it

the case that because those people speak ill of us
we should resort to doing untrue things and start
putting on a false front? No, absolutely not! We
should have our feet firmly planted on the ground,
and continue to do what is real and true. It
doesn't matter what type of demons come to the
City of Ten Thousand Buddhas; eventually they will
be subdued. No one can stir up trouble in the
Way Place, because if they do, they'll reap a bad
retribution. In cultivating the Way, you must
bring forth your true mind. It's not permissible
to fake it. Instead, you should have this attitude:

> Unchanging in the face of a
>   thousand demons;
> Non-retreating in the face of
>   ten thousand demons.

-excerpt from Instructional Talk
by Venerable Master Hua

CONTEMPLATIONS OF A FILIAL YOUTH

A Good Advisor is a door that tends toward All-Wisdom, for he enables me to enter the true and actual way. A Good Advisor is a vehicle that tends toward All-Wisdom, for he enables me to arrive at the ground of a Buddha. A Good Advisor is a boat that tends toward All-Wisdom, for he enables me to arrive at the jeweled continent of wisdom. A Good Advisor is a torch that tends toward All-Wisdom, for he enables me to produce the brightness of the Ten Powers. A Good Advisor is a road that tends toward All-Wisdom, for he enables me to enter the city of Nirvana. A Good Advisor is a lamp that tends toward All-Wisdom, for he enables me to recognize safe and perilous paths. A Good Advisor is a bridge that tends toward All-Wisdom, for he takes me across dangerous and evil places. A Good Advisor is a canopy that tends toward All-Wisdom, for he enables me to produce the coolness of great kindness. A Good Teacher is an eye that tends toward All-Wisdom, for he enables me to obtain the way to see the nature of all dharmas. A Good Teacher is a tide that tends toward All-Wisdom, for he fills me with the water of great compassion.

-excerpt from FLOWER ADORNMENT SUTRA, Entering the Dharma Realm, Part II.

THE BEGINNING OF FILIAL PIETY

Confucius sat at ease and Tseng Tzu attended upon him. The Master said, "The kings of old ruled the empire by means of perfect virtue and the essentials of the Way. The people were in harmony so that between high and low there was no quarreling. Did you know that?"

Tseng Tzu arose from his seat and said, "Shen is foolish, how could he have known?"

The Master said, "Filial piety is the root of all virtue and the origin of teaching. Be seated, and I shall tell you about it. The person, body, hair, and skin are given by the parents; one dare not harm them. This is the beginning of filial piety."

-The Classic of Filial Piety

* * *

The kindness of parents is as boundless as the sky, higher than heaven, and broader than the earth.

GIVING

There are three types of giving that bring
infinite rewards: giving to the sick, giving
to one's parents, and giving to the Thus Come Ones.

-excerpt from the
MAHAPARINIRVANA SUTRA

From a wise person I once heard these words:
I would rather be poked three hundred times every
day by sharp spears than to give rise to a single
bad thought toward my parents.

DIFFERENT WAYS TO SERVE ONE'S TEACHER

"You should bring forth the mind of being able to bring to maturity the different crops and grains, so that you can stoop to a lowly position. You should bring forth a mind of being like a good steed, so that you are able to be devoid of a vile nature. You should bring forth a mind of being like a huge carriage, so that you can transport a heavy load. You should bring forth a mind of being like a tamed elephant, so that you are constantly subdued. You should bring forth a mind of being like Mount Sumeru, so that you are not swayed or toppled. You should bring forth a mind of being like a faithful dog, so that you would never harm your Master. You should bring forth a mind of being like a Chandala, so that you are apart from conceit. You should bring forth a mind of being like a cow, so that you don't flare up in fierce rage. You should bring forth a mind of being like a ship's captain, in that in coming and going you never weary. You should bring forth a mind of being like a bridge, so that in ferrying across beings, you forget all about tiredness. You should bring forth a mind of being like a filial child,

so that you can serve your teacher according to the
expressions on his face. You should bring forth a
mind of being like a prince, in that you obey
instructions and commands.

FILIAL PIETY TOWARDS ONE'S TEACHER WHO IS A
GOOD KNOWING ADVISOR

The Youth Good Wealth single-mindedly recol-
lected how he should rely upon the Good Knowing
Advisor; how he should attend upon the Good Knowing
Advisor; how he should revere the Good Knowing
Advisor; how from the Good Knowing Advisor he could
behold All-Wisdom; how towards the Good Knowing
Advisor he should never be in opposition or be
rebellious; how towards the Good Knowing Advisor
he should not have any thoughts of flattery or de-
ceit; how towards the Good Knowing Advisor his
heart should always be in accord; how he should
regard the Good Knowing Advisor as a kind mother,
so as to renounce and separate from all unbeneficial
dharmas; how he should regard the Good Knowing
Advisor as a compassionate father, so as to give
rise to all good dharmas.

-excerpts from FLOWER ADORNMENT
SUTRA, Entering the Dharma
Realm, Part II.

THE FIVE MORAL OBLIGATIONS

When rulers are courteous and ministers are loyal,
When fathers are kind and their children filial,
When elder brothers are friendly,
  and younger brothers reverent,
When husbands and wives are mutually respectful,
And when friends treat each other
  with honesty and good faith,
The five moral obligations are established,
And all of society will prosper and thrive.

THE HIGHEST VIRTUE

Filiality is the natural course of those between
    heaven and earth.
A humane act inspires reciprocity and
    agrees with universal principle.
Utmost filiality is the foundation
    for the making of heroes and sages.
It is the epitome of the ten thousand virtues.

THE FOUR VIRTUES

A nation's wealth lies in its moral attitudes.
To cherish the people one begins by
  being filial to one's parents.
From filiality we proceed to develop
  loyalty to our leaders.
From loyalty, humaneness and righteousness
  come forth.
With these four virtues--filiality,
  loyalty, humaneness, and righteousness--
We're able to benefit humankind,
To change our evil ways,
And to return to what is proper and auspicious.

WHEN I SERVE MY PARENTS

When I serve my parents,

I vow that living beings

Will be skilled at serving the Buddhas

And will protect and nourish all.

-excerpt from FLOWER ADORNMENT SUTRA
"Pure Conduct," Chapter 11

THE BASIS OF HUMANITY

We living beings should be filial to our
parents, for those who are not filial commit offenses. Filial piety is important because it is
the basis of humanity; if people are not filial,
they forget their very origin. Therefore it is
said,

> Father gave me life, mother raised me;
> Their kindness--as vast as high heaven,
>   as manifold as the hairs on the head--
> Is difficult to repay.

What is filial piety? Does it mean buying good
food for one's parents to eat?   Is it perhaps
seeing that they are dressed in fine clothes? No.
These are outer forms of filial piety. The
innerworkings of filiality are to comply
with one's parents' basic concerns and ideas.

"Suppose my father likes to smoke opium. If
he smoked one ounce a day, then I should smoke two
in order to be compliant and filial, right?" No,
that would certainly not be filial conduct. When
I said "comply" I meant to comply with the basic
parental desire for their children's welfare, not
to comply with the parents' outer habits.

-excerpt from the EARTH STORE
BODHISATTVA SUTRA, commentary
by Venerable Master Hua

PARENTAL LOVE

Of all the kinds of love in the world, the strongest is parents' love for their children. No matter how bad a child may act towards his parents, they'll still forgive him. "He's just a child," they'll say. "He doesn't understand things." Even when a small child strikes his father or scolds his mother, the parents are accepting and don't feel that he has done anything wrong. Parents are like that because they love their children so much. The love of parents for their children is deeper and fiercer than the love between husband and wife.

THE BUDDHAS' LOVING PROTECTION

The Buddhas' loving protection for all living beings is like that of parents for their children, but even stronger yet. The love of Buddhas is a compassionate, universally pervasive love which protects all beings and causes their difficulties and problems to disappear. It is not the selfish, emotional love which most people experience. Take careful note of this point.

*—excerpt from SHURANGAMA SUTRA,
Volume One, commentary by
- Venerable Master Hua   .*

IF PEOPLE ARE NOT FILIAL

Earth Store Bodhisattva said to the Holy Mother,
"These are the names of the retributions for offenses in Jambudvipa (the continent where we live).
Living beings who are not filial to their parents,
who harm or kill them, will fall into the uninter-
rupted hell, where for thousands of millions of
kalpas they will seek in vain to escape."

-excerpt from the EARTH STORE
BODHISATTVA SUTRA.

* * *

If people are not filial to their parents,
they have not fulfilled the fundamental
responsibility of human beings. It is essential that people repay the enormous
kindness shown them by their parents.

* * *

THE POWER OF VOWS

Those who have lost their parents' devoted care,
And who do not know what paths their
    spirits took;
Or who have lost brothers, sisters, or
    other kin
At such an early age they never knew them well,
Should carve or paint an image of Earth
    Store Bodhisattva,
Should gaze at and worship him unceasingly.
For twenty-one days they should constantly
    hold his name,
After which, the Bodhisattva may reveal
    a boundless body
And show the realms in which the kin
    have been born.
Relatives who have fallen into evil ways,
Will quickly be able to leave those
    states of woe.

-excerpt from the EARTH STORE
BODHISATTVA SUTRA.

FIVE KINDS OF FILIAL PIETY

1. LIMITED FILIAL PIETY. This means being filial within one's own family, but not extending the virtue of filial piety beyond that.

2. EXTENSIVE FILIAL PIETY. This means one is able to "treat all elders as one's own; treat all children as one's own." With extensive filial piety one reaches throughout the world, taking all fathers and mothers in the world as one's own.

3. CONTEMPORARY FILIAL PIETY. This means one models oneself on present-day exemplars of filial piety and accords with present-day methods of making one's parents happy.

4. CLASSICAL FILIAL PIETY. This means to be filial to all the myriad creatures, in the same way that the Twenty-four Paragons of Filial Virtue were in Zhung Kuo.

5. ULTIMATE FILIAL PIETY. This means leaving the home-life just as Shakyamuni Buddha did. Although he appeared to go against his father's wishes by running away from the palace to cultivate the Way, ultimately, when he realized Buddhahood, he ascended to the heavens to speak Dharma for his

mother. Someone may ask, "But if one leaves home, one renounces one's family ties. How is that being filial?"

There's a saying:

When one child enters the Buddha's door,
Nine generations of ancestors ascend to the
heavens.

If you leave home and cultivate the Way, nine generations of ancestors receive the benefit and can ascend to the heavens. In that way, you are being filial, not only to your parents, but to your grandparents, your great grandparents, your great-great grandparents, and so on to seven generations of elders. But of course you must cultivate. The mere act of leaving home is not sufficiently powerful to cause your nine generations of relatives to be reborn in the heavens. If you do not cultivate the Way, they will not reap any benefit. But if you do cultivate, you are practicing great filial piety.

-excerpt from the EARTH STORE
BODHISATTVA SUTRA, commentary
by Venerable Master Hua

FILIAL SON PAI

When Master Hua was nineteen years old, his
mother died. After the funeral service, the other
relatives prepared to leave, but the Master sat
down on the bare ground by his mother's grave and
did not answer his brothers' taunting calls. The
family left without him, and he stayed on alone,
fasting through the night and the following day.
The second evening a pack of wolf dogs closed in
on him, but the Master was so intent upon his filial
practice that he refused to move in body or mind.
The pack, circling low and snarling, closed in
slowly until they were only a few feet away. Then
as if on signal, they all turned and ran off. Had
the Master started, the dogs would have pounced
at once, but because he did not move, they refrain-
ed from bothering him. From then on, although the
dogs chased off other visitors to the cemetery,
they never bothered anyone who came to see the
Master.

The Master left his mother's grave long enough
to go to San Yüan (Three Conditions) Monastery
at P'ing Fang Chan, south of the city of Harbin,

to receive the ten precepts of a Shramanera, thus
leaving the home-life. Then he returned to the
grave, resolved to watch over it for the three-
year mourning period traditional in Zhung Kuo.
He built a five-by-eight foot open-ended A-frame
hut from sorghum stalks, which did little to keep
out the elements. Clothed only in a rag robe,
he endured the Manchurian winters and the blazing
summer sun as he cultivated the concentrated
mindfulness of meditation, recited the name of
Amitabha Buddha, and recited the Sutras. He ate
only one meal a day at noon, always sat and never
lay down to sleep, and compassionately offered
healing protection to many people. Occasionally
he would enter samadhi for weeks at a time, never
rising from his seat. By the time he had completed
the three-year mourning period, the Master had been
visited by over two thousand people including
scholars, farmers, workers, merchants, and officials.

One night near the end of the three years,
the residents of the nearby village saw that the
Master's hut was on fire. A brilliant light shot

up ten yards into the air and the area around the
hut was as bright as broad daylight. Many people
rushed to the graveyard, crying, "The filial son's
hut has caught fire!" Soon there were hundreds
of people there with buckets of water to lend
assistance. When they arrived, however, they
found the tiny hut as peaceful as always; the
Master was sitting absorbed in meditation.

One day while sitting in meditation the Master
saw the Venerable Master Hui Neng, the Sixth
Patriarch, who lived during the T'ang dynasty,
enter his hut. The Patriarch spoke with him for
a long time. "In the future you will go to the
West. The five schools will divide into ten,"
he told the Master, "in order to teach and transform endless hundreds of thousands of living beings,
as countless as sands in the Ganges River. It will
be the beginning of the Buddhadharma in the West."
Afterwards, the Master rose to accompany the
Patriarch out of the hut. Only after the Sixth
Patriarch had taken four or five steps and suddenly disappeared did the Master remember that the
Patriarch had entered Nirvana more than eleven
hundred years before!

LU CHI, WHO KEPT ORANGES TO TAKE HOME TO HIS MOTHER

Lu Chi lived during the time of the Three Kingdoms Period in the state of Wu. His father, named Lu K'ang, was a magistrate at the end of the Han dynasty. Lu K'ang was extremely filial from a very early age, and his son, Lu Chi, was profoundly influenced by his father's example and also became a very filial son.

When Lu Chi was six years old, his father took him to visit Governor Yüan Shu of Nan Yang. One of Yüan Shu's servants offered Lu Chi some oranges. After he had eaten two, he took three more and hid them in the sleeve of his robe. He then played for a while, and when it was time to go home, he bowed respectfully to the Governor. But as he bent over to bow, the oranges fell out of his sleeve and rolled around on the floor.

When Yüan Shu saw them, he laughed, (for Lu Chi was still very young) and said, "You've come here as my young guest. Is it right to steal my oranges?"

Lu Chi knelt on the floor and said, "Please, Sir, I didn't take them for myself. Oranges are my mother's favorite fruit. I only wanted to take these home for her to eat. Please forgive me."

When Governor Yüan Shu realized that, young
as he was, Lu Chi already knew how to be filial
to his mother, he praised him and gave him a whole
box of oranges to take home to his mother.

Once the military strategist Sun Tse and
his friends were discussing the world situation.
They decided that things were too disorderly and
chaotic and that they would have to take matters
into their own hands. Although Lu Chi was still
very young at the time, he was sitting at the
back of the room and heard the conversation. When
he heard what they had said he disagreed and spoke
up in a loud voice: "In the past when the Great
Duke Huan of Ch'i was ruling, he didn't use armies
to control people. We have to change people's
hearts so that they want to serve their country.
How can you use force to rule people? Although
I'm very young, I can see that this is completely
wrong!" The group of people he was addressing
felt that what he said had principle and realized
that it was rare indeed for such a young child
to have so much insight.

When Lu Chi grew up, he became a great schola

He served both as a prefect and an army general.
The maps he made of the constellations were a
significant contribution to science. Alas, he
died too soon! When he was but thirty-two years
old, he left the world.

People of the world praise him with the
following verse:

Filiality and fraternal respect
    were his heavenly nature,
This boy of merely six years.
In his sleeve he hid oranges
    for his mother,
As a token of his deep devotion.

TSENG SHEN, WHO FELT PAIN HIMSELF WHEN HIS MOTHER BIT HER FINGER

Tseng Shen lived during the Western Chou
dynasty in the country of Lü. He was a disciple of
Confucius and was always extremely filial to his
parents. One day Tseng Shen was helping his father
weed in the fields. The child accidently pulled
up some melon plants. His mistake enraged his
father, who got so angry he lost his wits and
picked up a wooden club. Letting loose a great
blow, he hit Tseng Shen full force. Wanting to be
compliant, the child just stood there to receive
the punishment, but his father's swing was so
powerful that the blow from the club knocked the
boy unconscious. Realizing what he had done, his
father got quite anxious. But after a while,
Tseng Shen regained consciousness and not only was
he not the least bit unhappy with his father for
having struck him, he knelt before him and asked
forgiveness for his mistake. Despite his father's
tremendous anger and heavy blow, Tseng Shen was
able to sing and clap his hands in an attempt to
cheer his father up.

When Confucius heard about the incident, he admonished Tseng Shen, saying, "If your father hits you with his hand to punish you, then you certainly must take it respectfully. But if your father uses a club and beats you with too much force, you must try to avoid the blows. That is because if your father, in a fit of anger, inflicts such harm on you to the point that you die, then wouldn't you have caused your parents anguish and placed them in a position where they would be subject to great malice? Were that to happen, you would not be acting as a filial son." After hearing his teacher's instruction, Tseng Shen knelt before Confucius and thanked him for the lesson.

After Tseng Shen's father died, life was very difficult for his mother and him. Each day Tseng Shen had to go up into the mountains and down to the fields to work, as well as to return home and care for his aging mother. One time when Tseng Shen was in the mountains cutting firewood, a guest came to his home. His mother was the only one there. There was no money in the house and she was not able to go out by herself to buy things, so she felt very anxious about not being able to entertain

the guest properly. She wished her son would come
home soon, but still he didn't come. Finally,
she thought to herself, "Tseng Shen is usually
such a filial, obedient son. He always feels what
I feel. If I bite down on my finger, for sure,
up in the mountains my son will feel my pain."
So she bit down hard on her finger until it bled.

Exactly at that moment, Tseng Shen felt a
pain in his heart and knew that there must be a
problem at home. So he quickly gathered up his
things and returned home. When he arrived, he
knelt in the doorway and asked his mother what
had caused the pain in his heart. When his mother
explained what she had done, he understood why
he had felt the pain and he quickly put down the
wood and went to take care of the guest.

Tseng Shen's mother believed in her son so
completely that nothing could convince her that
he could do bad things. One day when she was
weaving at her loom a man came running by yelling,
"Tseng Shen killed a man! Tseng Shen killed a
man!" But she didn't even turn her head.

A little while later another person came
along again shouting, "Tseng Shen killed a man!"

This time Tseng Shen's mother looked up for a
second, but then went back to her work. Yet again,
a while later, another person came to tell her that
Tseng Shen had killed a man, but his mother still
didn't believe him. She did put down her work
and go outside to see what was happening, however.
But she found out that it was another person named
Tseng Shen who had killed a man--not her own son.

When Tseng Shen heard about this, he was even
more careful only to do what was right and never
to do what was wrong. Each day he examined himself
on three points: "Have I been faithful in my
dealings with others? Have I been trustworthy
to my friends? Have I mastered and practiced the
instructions of my teacher?" Because of this kind
of sincerity and diligence, he was able to become
a great sage.

After Confucius died, Tseng Shen, also called
Tseng Tzu, transmitted his teacher's teachings to
others. He then gave his position to Tzu Ssu, who
then passed it on to Mencius. At the time of Mencius, the Confucianists established a groundwork
for moral and ethical behavior that influenced
the culture for thousands of years. Besides

transmitting his teacher's philosophy, Tseng Tzu
also wrote a commentary on THE GREAT LEARNING,
one of the FOUR BOOKS, as well as the CLASSIC OF
FILIAL PIETY. Both of these great philosophical
works are esteemed by people to this very day.
You could say that Tseng Shen was a most outstand-
ing filial son among filial sons, and a teacher
and model for all future generations.

A verse was written in praise of his filial
deeds.

When his mother bit into her finger,
The son couldn't bear the pain in his heart.
Carrying firewood he returned at once,
How deep the bonds between flesh and blood!

LADY T'ANG WHO GAVE HER MILK WITHOUT CEASE

During the T'ang dynasty, there was a man
named Ts'ui Nan-shan who lived under one roof with
the members of his extended family, including his
grandmother, great grandmother, their children,
and their grandchildren. His great-grandmother's
name was Ch'ang Sun and so she was called Great
Lady Ch'ang Sun. His grandmother's name was T'ang
and she was called Lady T'ang.

Great Lady Ch'ang Sun was very old and un-
steady when she walked. Although she had a cane,
she still needed someone to help her get around.
Also, she had no teeth and so she couldn't chew
her food. An old person in such condition needed
a tremendous amount of care in order to stay alive.

Ts'ui Nan-shan's grandmother, Lady T'ang was
an extremely filial woman and also a virtuous and
pure daughter-in-law. When she was still a young
woman, she was afraid her mother-in-law would not
get enough nourishment since she had no teeth
with which to chew her food, so each morning Lady
T'ang would go to her mother-in-law's room and give
the elderly woman her own milk to drink as

nourishment. Not only that, she also would take
Great Lady Ch'ang Sun out for walks each day so
that she could get some fresh air and exercise.
This went on for several years during which Great
Lady Ch'ang Sun was very healthy.

Finally, though, the day came when she felt
quite weak and realized that her life was coming
to an end. On her death bed, she called all her
children and grandchildren to her, as well as her
daughter-in-law. When they had all assembled, she
spoke to them with what little life-breath she
had remaining, "Because I am old and have no
teeth to chew my food, nor strong legs to walk on,
I have been totally dependent on my daughter-in-
law. She has given me milk and cared for me in
such a way that I have been able to live on through
many more years than I might have. But now even
that won't help me. There is no way for me to
repay the kindness and virtue of my daughter-in-law.
but I do have a wish I want to express. I hope
that all of you, my children and grandchildren,
will be as filial to your elders as she has been
to me. If you can be so, then I can die in peace."

After she had finished speaking, Great Lady

Ch'ang Sun passed away. All of her children and grandchildren were extremely moved by Lady T'ang's devotion and they, in turn, did their very best to always be filial and respectful to their elders. The neighbors and citizens in the area surrounding their home soon heard of Lady T'ang's filial devotion, and it became a household saying that if you wish to have filial children and grandchildren, then you must first be filial to your own elders. A poem was written to tell future generations about Lady T'ang.

> The lady of the house of Ts'ui
>   was filial and respectful.
> In the morning after washing up and combing
>   her hair, she gave milk from her own body.
> That kindness her mother-in-law
>   couldn't repay.
> So the Great Lady hoped her sons and
>   grandsons would be equally filial.

射狼當道荊棘叢
下邳孝子作富公
負母避賊竟
逢賊賊人不殺
江次翁
五是大孝子
殺者非英雄
嗚呼
賊人殺人
直如戲次翁
不殺亦天意
江革行
庸供母

CHIANG KE, WHO LABORED FOR HIS MOTHER

In the late Han period (75-219 A.D.) there
was a filial son whose name was Chiang Ke. He was
a citizen of Lin Tzu in the Kingdom of Ch'i. When
he was very young his father died leaving only
his mother and himself. At that time the "Yellow
Kerchief" bandits were in revolt and they pilfered
and looted, causing great disorder and chaos. The
good citizens who couldn't protect themselves
formed groups and left the area. Chiang Ke's
mother was quite old and weak and couldn't stand
the fright and agitation. So, in order to try
and protect his mother from the thieves, he carried
her on his back and left their village to find
another place to live.

Traveling was extremely difficult. There
was nothing to eat and so they lived on whatever
wild fruit and vegetables they could find. The
greatest problem, however, was the gangs of thieves
and bandits. Usually when the bandits caught
sight of Chiang Ke and his mother they saw them
as a poor old mother and her son who had nothing
worth stealing, so they left them alone. But
there were other groups of strong young men who

wanted to capture Chiang Ke and force him to work
for their gangs. When this happened, Chiang Ke
would kneel in front of them and weep, begging
for mercy and saying, "Please, sirs, if I go with
you, my old mother will have no one to care for
her. Please allow us to go on our way."

All the bandits would be moved by the sincerity and earnestness of such a filial son, for even
bandits have parents. So, upon remembering their
own mothers, they would feel compassion and allow
the two to go.

Undergoing limitless suffering and difficulty,
the boy and his mother passed through the lawless
land of thieves and bandits and reached K'an Pi
county in Chiang Su region. As a result of their
ordeal, they were in rags and had no money at all.
Chiang Ke walked barefoot without even a shirt on
his back to earn money to provide food and clothing
for his mother. He undertook heavy menial tasks.

Whenever Chiang Ke made some money working as
a laborer, he would first bring it home and offer
it as a gift to his mother. He made sure she had
everything she needed: food, clothing, and medicine. But he couldn't bring himself to buy such

things for himself. He even went without shoes.
To his mother, he gave the finest foods, but he
ate only the coarsest kinds himself. His filial
devotion inspired the people in the village where
he lived and they took up a collection to help
the boy and his mother. In this way the two were
able to survive in this village far from their
home.

When peace came again to their native land,
Chiang Ke and his mother returned to their home
town. But because his mother was so old, she
couldn't take the rough ride in a horse drawn cart.
So Chiang Ke pulled the cart himself, all the way
home.

Everyone praised him and called him "Filial
Hero Chiang." Everywhere, people heard stories
of his filial deeds and grew to respect him.
Even government officials offered him gifts and
asked him to work for the country and the people.
But, because his mother was so old, Chiang Ke
felt he needed to care for her. He amiably thanked
the people for their good intentions, but refused
their offers to change his lifestyle. Out of respect and admiration, people composed a poem about
him which says:

With his mother on his back,
  he escaped through dangers and difficulties.
Although proverty-stricken,
  they were harassed by thieves.
He asked for pity and each time
  gained reprieve,
As he worked always to provide
  for his mother.

MENG TSUNG, WHO SHED TEARS WHICH CAUSED BAMBOO SHOOTS TO SPROUT UP FROM THE FROZEN EARTH

Meng Tsung, also called Kung Wu, lived during the Three Kingdoms Period and was from the region of Chiang Hsia. When he was young, he studied with Li Su of Nan Yang. His mother made him a huge quilt and when people saw it they thought it strange that she would make such a big quilt for such a small boy. His mother explained, "We are a very poor family and don't have enough money to buy bedding for Kung Wu's guests. I made this huge quilt so that they can all sleep together under one covering and be close friends."

Meng Tsung worked very hard at his studies and often stayed up studying until dawn. His teacher, Li Su, always praised him and said, "In the future you will go from being an ordinary official to become Prime Minister."

Later when the child grew up, he worked for the General of Sung. He and his mother lived in an army barracks nearby. One night it rained and the roof of the barracks leaked. The more Meng Tsung thought about his mother sleeping under a leaking

roof, the worse he felt. Finally, in the middle
of the night he went to his mother and cried, "I
didn't fix the roof. I'm truly sorry. Now you have
to suffer because of my negligence."

His mother replied, "What's the use of crying? Just work harder in the future. How is crying
going to fix the roof?"

One winter his mother suddenly started craving
bamboo shoots. In those days you couldn't just go
to the store and buy a can of them. In the spring
they were harvested from the bamboo grove, but
in the dead of winter, where could one find sprout-
ing bamboo? Not knowing what to do, but wanting
to make his mother happy, Meng Tsung went to a
nearby bamboo grove. There, he paced back and
forth extremely disraught and agitated. Finally,
he knelt in the snow and began to cry. Though
it may seem strange, just at the moment his tears
hit the ground, the frozen earth broke open and
bamboo shoots appeared. He quickly gathered them
up and took them home to give to his mother to eat
Later, when people heard about this, they knew
that his sincere filial intentions moved heaven
and earth to help him.

Eventually, even Emperor Wu came to hear of Meng Tsung's filial conduct, and made him Keeper of the Royal Fish Ponds. He was responsible for raising the fish, making the nets, catching the fish, and preserving them. Always thinking of his mother's welfare, he sent some preserved fish home to her. Much to his surprise, his mother sent them back with the following message: "You are Keeper of the Royal Fish Ponds. If you send the Emperor's preserved fish home to me, aren't you afraid you will be accused of corruption? You should be careful to avoid suspicion!"

When he became the Prefect for the State of Wu and had duties which prevented him from being able to go home to see his mother, he would save up all the good food offered to him to eat and send it home to her. One day Meng Tsung's mother suddenly became ill and died. When he received the news, he dropped everything and returned home to mourn for her. According to the laws of his time, he could have been put to death for leaving his post.

After observing the proper rites of mourning, he went to the government and turned himself in.

At that time a great official in the government spoke in his behalf, pointing out that his conduct had at all other times been beyond reproach. In light of that, he requested that the authorities not punish him too severely.

As a result of that official's testimony, a proclamation was issued stating that due to unavoidable circumstances, Meng Tseng had to leave his post temporarily, and therefore was pardoned of any offense. The statement added that he should, however, not make a practice of it. Shortly thereafter, he returned to his post. Meng Tsung was truly a filial son!

Inspired by Meng Tsung's filial conduct, those of the world composed a verse in praise of him:

In the desolate cold of winter,
    his filial tears fell
Upon a few bare and frozen
    bamboo stalks.
In an instant, new shoots sprouted--
A sign of divine approval,
    heralding peace and joy.

TS'AI HSUN, WHO COLLECTED MULBERRIES
TO GIVE TO HIS MOTHER

In the time of the Eastern Han Dynasty, there
lived a young, filial boy, whose surname was Ts'ai
Tan, and whose personal name was Tso Hsun. When
he was very young, his father died, leaving him
and his mother alone to make ends meet.

Ts'ai Hsun served his mother joyfully and was
extremely filial, and so all the neighboring people
were very fond of him. But this was a time of
political upheaval. There were those who were
plotting against the throne, hoping to make themselves Emperor. Because of this, thieves and bandits descended like a plague of locusts, setting
fires and wreaking havoc. They were reckless and
bold, so the people lived in a state of constant
anxiety. Moreover, a famine continued from year
to year, making the lives of the citizens worse
each day.

Because he wanted to serve his mother, Ts'ai
Hsun would go into the wilderness each day to pick
mulberries for their meal, and then bring them
back to give to his old mother.

When Ts'ai Hsun went berry picking, he always
brought along two baskets. He put the ripe, black
berries he picked into one basket and the sour, red
ones into the other basket.

One day, just when Ts'ai Hsun was out picking
berries, there suddenly appeared a gang of red-
browed bandits, whose name came from the red paint

they smeared on their brows.   They saw Ts'ai Hsun
picking mulberries, carefully separating them into
two baskets, and they thought it very strange. So,
very brashly and rudely they asked him, "Little
brother, you haven't picked very many mulberries.
Why do you need two baskets? Wouldn't one be more
than enough?"

Ts'ai Hsun replied, "Because the black mulberries are ripe, they have a sweet taste and these I
give to my mother to eat. The red mulberries are
not ripe yet, and so they are sour. Those I eat
myself. For this reason, I divide them into two
different baskets."

When the red-browed bandits heard Ts'ai Hsun's
explanation, they were very much impressed. In
their hearts they compared themselves to this very
young boy who was already so filial and were very
ashamed. "We have deserted our parents to become
thieves. We don't even measure up to a child,"
they thought to themselves.

Then, those red-browed bandits suddenly grew
kind and offered Ts'ai Hsun three bags of rice and
some beef to take home to his mother. But, Ts'ai
Hsun said, "Mama told me that I shouldn't want
things that belong to others. Since these things
you want to give me have been stolen from other
people, I am even less able to take them."

When the thieves heard this, they were moved
to shame and each one said, "Thank you, little
brother, for your precious good words. Originally

we, too, were good sons and brothers, but we came
under the influence of modern times. We wish to
return to our families, take care of our parents,
and no longer be bad."

There is a saying that "When the heart is
sincere, even metal and stone can be penetrated."
If one has a completely true, devoted, and filial
mind, one can move even a hard-hearted thief.

Ts'ai Hsun's filial devotion not only impressed
the bandits, but the story of his filial conduct
changed the entire village he lived in to a
place of propriety. In order to praise his virtue,
a poem was written that goes like this:

> The black mulberries he gave to his mother,
> Though he himself wept tears of
>   hunger and sorrow.
> The red-browed recognized his filial
>   devotion,
> And offered him a present of rice and
>   beef.

Life at
the City of
Ten Thousand
Buddhas

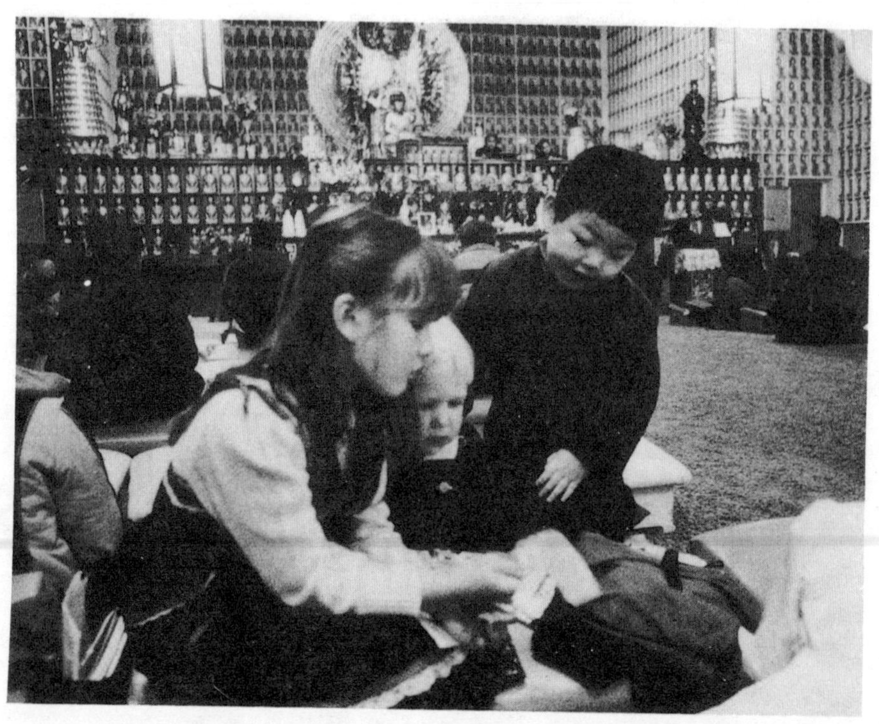

Children are encouraged to share the sweet lessons provided
by the unsurpassed Dharma, but in no way do the schools of
the Sagely City use manipulative techniques to convert
its students to Buddhism.

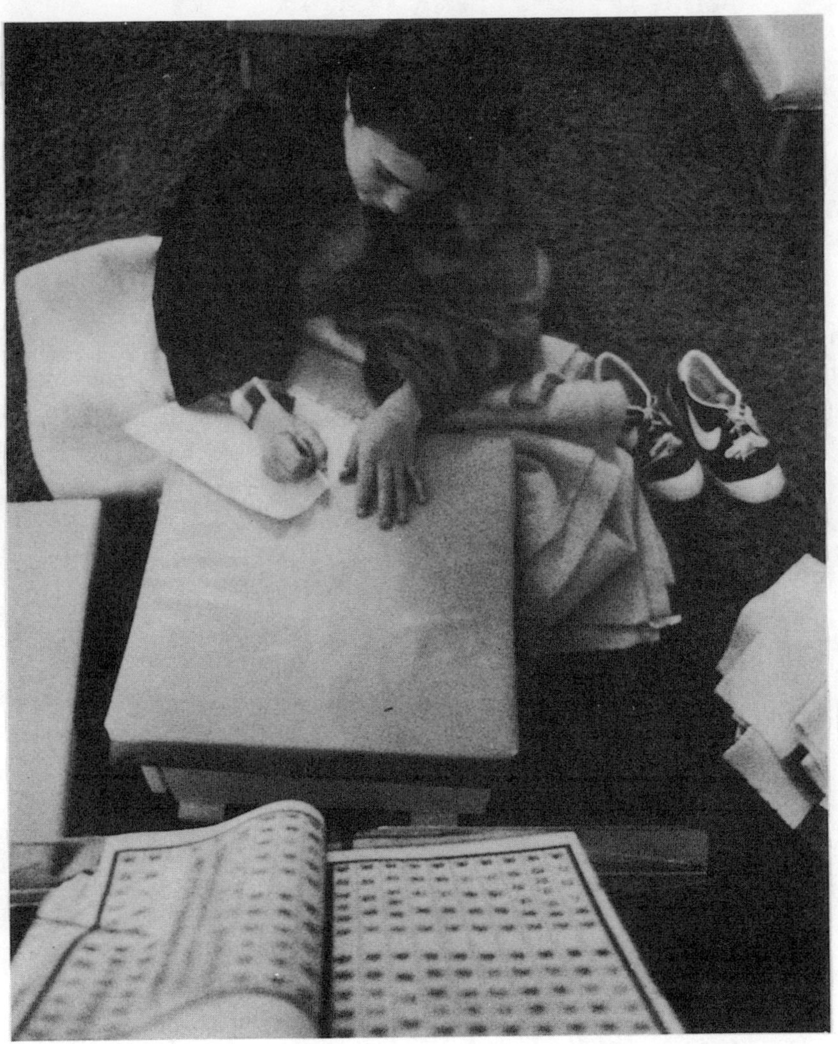

Following an ancient method of study, a young disciple of the Buddha copies out and commits to memory passages of the Buddhist scriptures:

> Seeking all the various Sutra texts,
> Their minds are never weary or fatigued.
> Well can they understand their drift
>   and meaning,
> And apply them to their practice
>   in this world.
>
> —Ten Grounds Chapter 26
> FLOWER ADORNMENT SUTRA

At Instilling Virtue Girls' School a primary empha-
sis is placed on helping students learn to be filial
children, loyal citizens, and virtuous people of the
world.

Students from the Buddhist Council for Refugee
Rescue and Resettlement also enroll in the grade
and high schools. They are taught English and other
life skills to facilitate their adjustment to a
new culture and environment.

Students of all ages and different national and ethnic backgrounds live together under the Five Great Principles of the Sagely City: no greed, no fighting, no seeking, no selfishness, and no pursuit of self-benefit.

Carpentry and other applied arts are part of the
rigorous training program for all high school students.

THE BUDDHIST TEXT TRANSLATION SOCIETY

CHAIRPERSON: The Venerable Tripitaka Master Hsüan Hua
                -Abbot of Gold Mountain Monastery, Gold
                  Wheel Monastery, and Tathagata Monastery
                -Chancellor of Dharma Realm Buddhist
                  University
                -Professor of the Tripitaka and the Dhyanas

PRIMARY TRANSLATION COMMITTEE:

Chairpersons: Venerable Tripitaka Master Hsüan Hua
               Bhikshuni Heng Ch'ih

Members:

Bhikshu Heng Sure   Bhikshuni Heng Tao
Bhikshu Heng Kuan   Bhikshuni Heng Ming
Bhikshu Heng Shun   Bhikshuni Heng Hsien
Bhikshu Heng Ch'au   Bhikshuni Heng Tsai
Bhikshu Heng Tso   Bhikshuni Heng Duan
Bhikshu Heng Ch'i   Bhikshuni Heng Bin
Bhikshu Heng Gung   Bhikshuni Heng Liang
Bhikshu Heng Wu   Bhikshuni Heng Lyan
Bhikshu Heng Jau   Bhikshuni Heng Chia
Bhikshu Heng Ch'ang   Upasika Terri Nicholson
                           Upasaka David Rounds
Bhikshuni Heng Ch'ing   Upasaka R. B. Epstein
Bhikshuni Heng Chü   Upasaka Chou Li-jen
Bhikshuni Heng Chai   Upasika Janice V. Storss
Bhikshuni Heng Wen

REVIEWING COMMITTEE:

Chairpersons: Bhikshu Heng Tso
               Upasaka Kuo Jung Epstein

Members:

Bhikshu Heng Sure   Bhikshuni Heng Hsien
Bhikshu Heng Kuan   Bhikshuni Heng Tsai
Bhikshu Heng Gung   Bhikshuni Heng Duan
Bhikshu Heng Wu   Bhikshuni Heng Bin
Bhikshuni Heng Ch'ih   Bhikshuni Heng Liang
Bhikshuni Heng Chai   Upasika Hsien Ping-ying
Bhikshuni Heng Wen   Upasaka David Rounds
Bhikshuni Heng Tao   Upasaka Chou Li-jen
                           Upasika Terri Nicholson

EDITING COMMITTEE:

Chairperson: Upasika Susan Rounds

Advisor: Bhikshu Heng Kuan

Members:

Bhikshu Heng Sure
Bhikshu Heng Lai
Bhikshu Heng Shun
Bhikshu Heng Ch'au
Bhikshu Heng Tso
Bhikshu Heng Ch'i
Bhikshu Heng Wu
Bhikshu Heng Jau
Bhikshuni Heng Ch'ih
Bhikshuni Heng Ch'ing
Bhikshuni Heng Chü
Bhikshuni Heng Chai
Bhikshuni Heng Wen
Bhikshuni Heng Tao
Bhikshuni Heng Ming
Bhikshuni Heng Hsien

Bhikshuni Heng Tsai
Bhikshuni Heng Duan
Bhikshuni Heng Bin
Bhikshuni Heng Liang
Bhikshuni Heng Lyan
Bhikshuni Heng Chia
Upasaka R.B. Epstein
Upasaka David Rounds
Upasika Nancy Lethcoe
Upasika Terri Nicholson
Upasaka Chou Li-jen
Upasika Phuong Kuo Wu
Upasika Janice V. Storss
Upasaka Douglas Powers
Upasika Marion Robertson
Upasika Marla Wong

CERTIFYING COMMITTEE:

Chairperson: Venerable Tripitaka Master Hsüan Hua

Members:

Bhikshu Heng Sure
Bhikshu Heng Kuan
Bhikshu Heng Tso
Bhikshuni Heng Ch'ih
Bhikshuni Heng Ch'ing
Bhikshuni Heng Wen

Bhikshuni Heng Tao
Bhikshuni Heng Hsien
Upasaka Wong Kuo Chün
Upasika Terri Nicholson
Upasaka R.B. Epstein
Upasika Janice V. Storss

CHINESE PUBLICATIONS COMMITTEE:

Chairperson: Upasaka Chou Li-jen

Members:

Bhikshuni Heng Lyan
Upasika Phuong Kuo Wu
Upasika Yao-sen Epstein

Bina Teng
Wong Kuo Ch'ang

All of the translation works by the Buddhist Text Translation Society are accompanied by interlinear commentaries by the Venerable Tripitaka Master Hsüan Hua, and are available in softcover only, unless otherwise noted.

BUDDHIST SUTRAS

Amitabha Sutra - This Sutra, which was spoken by the Buddha without being formally requested as in other Sutras, explains the causes and circumstances for rebirth in the Land of Ultimate Bliss of Amitabha (Limitless Light) Buddha. The commentary includes extensive information on common Buddhist terminology, and stories on many of the Buddha's foremost disciples. ISBN 0-917512-01-4, 204 pgs., $8.00 (Also available in Spanish. $8.00)

Brahma Net Sutra　梵網經講錄　The Buddha explains the Ten Major and Forty-eight Minor Precepts of the Bodhisattva. Bi-lingual edition, English-Zhung Wen.Vol. 1, ISBN 0-917512-79-0, 300 pgs. Vol. 2, ISBN 0-917512-88-X, 210 pgs. Two volume set is $18.00. The commentary to this work is·by the late Venerable Master Hui Seng.

Dharani Sutra - This Sutra tells of the past causes and conditions of the Bodhisattva of Great Compassion, Avalokiteshvara (Kuan Yin), and the various ways of practicing the Great Compassion Mantra. It is a fundamental Secret School text. The second half of the publication is divided up into three sections. The first explains the meaning of·the mantra line by line. The second has Zhung Wen poems and drawings of division bodies of Kuan Yin Bodhisattva for each of the 84 lines of the mantra. The last section contains drawings and verses in English on each of the 42 Hands and Eyes of Kuan Yin. This is the first English translation of this scripture. ISBN 0-917512-13-8, 352 pgs., $12.00

大悲心陀羅尼經　has all of the material noted above for the DHARANI SUTRA, except the commentary and the section explaining the meaning of the mantra. All the material is in Zhung Wen only.210 pgs., $6.00.

Dharma Flower (Lotus) Sutra - In this Sutra, which was spoken in the last period of the Buddha's teaching, the Buddha proclaims the ultimate principles of the Dharma which unites all previous teachings into one. When completed, the entire Sutra will be from 15 to 20 volumes. The following are those volumes which have been published to date:

Volume I, Introductory section. Discusses the five periods and eight teachings of the T'ien T'ai School and then analyzes the School's Five Profound Meanings as they relate to the Sutra. The last portion tells of the life of Tripitaka Master Kumarajiva, who translated the Sutra from Sanskrit to Zhung Wen. ISBN 0-917512-16-2, 85 pgs., $3.95

Volume II, Introduction, Chapter One. Describes the setting for the Sutra, which includes the assembly that gathered to hear it, the Buddha's emission of light, the questioning of Maitreya Bodhisattva, and the response given by Manjushri Bodhisattva. ISBN 0-917512-22-1, 324 pgs., $7.95

Volume III, Expedient Methods, Chapter Two. After the Buddha emerges from samadhi he speaks of the vast merit and virtue of the Buddhas. Shariputra beseeches him to expound further on this. After his third request, the Buddha consents, and for the first time proclaims that all beings without exception can become Buddhas. ISBN 0-917512-26-X, 183 pgs., $7.95

Volume IV, A Parable, Chapter Three. The Buddha explains the purpose of his teachings by means of an analogy of an Elder who tries to rescue five hundred children who are absorbed in play in a burning house. ISBN 0-917-512-62-6, 371 pgs., $8.95

Volume V, Belief and Understanding, Chapter Four. Four of the Buddha's foremost Arhat disciples relate a parable about a prodigal son to express their joy that they too, will become Buddhas. ISBN 0-917512-64-2, 200 pgs., $6.95

Volume VI, Medicinal Herbs, Chapter Five, & Conferring Predictions, Chapter Six. The Buddha uses the analogy of a rain-cloud to illustrate how his teaching benefits all beings. ISBN 0-917-512-65-0, 161 pgs., $6.95

Volume VII, Parable of the Transformation City, Chapter Seven. The Buddha teaches that the attainment of his Arhat disciples is like a city which he conjured up as an expedient when they became weary of the journey to Buddhahood. ISBN 0-917-512-93-6, 250 pgs., $7.95

Volume VIII, Five Hundred Disciples Receive Predictions, Chapter Eight, & Bestowing Predictions Upon Those Studying and Beyond Study, Chapter Nine. More than a thousand disciples receive predictions that they will become Buddhas in the future. ISBN 0-917-512-71-5, 160 pgs., $6.95

Volume IX, Masters of the Dharma, Chapter Ten & Vision of the Jewelled Stupa, Chapter Eleven. Chapter Ten explains the vast merit from upholding and propagating the LOTUS SUTRA, and in Chapter Eleven, all the transformation bodies of Shakyamuni Buddha gather so that those in the assembly can see Many Jewels Buddha. ISBN 0-917-512-85-5, 270 pgs., $9.00

Volume X, Devadatta, Chapter Twelve & Exhortation to Maintain, Chapter Thirteen. In Chapter Twelve, the Buddha reveals that Devadatta was once his teacher in a former life and then bestows a prediction of Buddhahood on him. The eight year old dragon girl becomes a Buddha. In Chapter Thirteen, the Buddha bestows predictions of Buddhahood on Bhikshunis. ISBN 0-88139-34-0, 150 pgs., $5.00

Volume XI, Peaceful & Happy Conduct, Chapter Fourteen. Elucidates the "places of closeness" that a Bodhisattva should draw near to and places he should stay apart from. Discusses the body, mouth, and mind karma of cultivators and the importance of vows. ISBN 0-88139-022-4.

Universal Door Chapter. Zhung Wen. $5.00
妙法蓮華經觀世音菩薩普門品淺釋

Flower Adornment (Avatamsaka) Sutra   大方廣佛華嚴經淺釋
Known as the 'King of Kings' of all Buddhist scriptures because of
its profundity and great length (81 rolls containing more than
700,000 Zhung Wen characters).It contains the most complete explanation of the Buddha's state and the Bodhisattva's quest for Awakening. When completed, the entire Sutra-text with commentary, is
estimated to be from 75 to 100 volumes. The following are those
volumes which have been published to date:

Verse Preface   華嚴經疏序淺釋   a succinct and eloquent verse
commentary by T'ang Dynasty National Master Ch'ing Liang who was
the Master of seven emperors. The Preface gives a complete explanation of all the fundamental principles contained in the Sutra.
This is the first English translation of this text. Bi-lingual edition, English & Zhung Wen.ISBN 0-917512-28-6, 244 pgs., $7.00

Prologue - a detailed explanation of the principles of the Sutra by
National Master Ch'ing Liang, utilizing the Hsien Shou method of
analyzing scriptures known as the Ten Doors. The PROLOGUE con-
tains the first Nine Doors. Will be approximately 7 to 10 volumes
upon completion. The following volumes have been published to date:
     First Door, The Causes and Conditions for the Arisal of the
Teaching of the FLOWER ADORNMENT SUTRA. Complete in one volume.
ISBN 0-917512-66-9, 252 pgs., $10.00
     Second Door, The Stores and Teachings in Which It (THE
FLOWER ADORNMENT SUTRA) is contained, in three volumes:

     Part One, Complete discussion of Three Stores; beginning
of discussion of the Schools in Zhung Kuo. ISBN 0-917512-73-1,
280 pgs., $10.00
     Part Two, More on Zhung Wen Schools. The Indian Schools,
and comparisons among them. ISBN 0-917512-98-7, 220 pgs., $10.00
     Part Three, Detailed discussion of the Five Hsien Shou
Teachings. The sequence of the Teaching Methods, and the incon-
ceivable state of the Flower Adornment. ISBN 0-88139-009-7, 160
pgs., $8.00

     華嚴經疏淺釋   the entire text and commentary of the Ten
Doors in Zhung Wen.Four volume set, $27.00

     Flower Store Adorned Sea of Worlds, Chapter 5, Part 1. De-
scribes the universe we live in, including an explanation of principles pertaining to the coming into being of worlds, the wind
wheels that uphold them, their orbits, mutual attraction, and detailed descriptions of the worlds located on the 20 tiers of the
lotus that forms the basis of our cosmic structure. ISBN 0-917512-
54-5, 250 pgs. $8.50

The Names of the Thus Come Ones, Chapter 7. In this chapter, the Bodhisattvas gather from the worlds of the ten directions to request the Buddha to speak about the Great Bodhisattva practices which are explained at great length in later chapters of the FLOWER ADORNMENT SUTRA. This volume also includes Chapter 8, The Four Holy Truths. Each of the Four Holy Truths--Suffering, Accumulation, Extinction, and the Way--are explained according to the conditions of ten different worlds plus the Saha World, the world which we inhabit. ISBN 0-88139-014-3.

Bright Enlightenment, Chapter 9. Shakyamuni Buddha emits light from the soles of his feet which continually gets brighter and shines upon more and different countries in the ten directions. After each time that he emits light, Manjushri Bodhisattva speaks verses praising the virtues of the Buddha. ISBN 0-88139-005-4, 225 pgs., $8.50

Pure Conduct, Chapter 11. This chapter of the Sutra gives a detailed explanation of the pure practices of the Bodhisattva. It is one of the most renowned guides to the Vinaya in the Buddhist Canon. ISBN 0-917512-37-5, 255 pgs., $9.00

Ten Dwellings, Chapter 15. Explains the state of the Ten Dwellings attained by the Bodhisattva. ISBN 0-917512-77-4, 185 pgs., $8.00

Brahma Conduct, Chapter 16. Explains the meanings of the pure Brahma conduct cultivated by the Bodhisattva. ISBN 0-917512-80-4, 65 pgs., $4.00

The Merit and Virtue From First Bringing Forth The Mind, Chapter 17. Uses various analogies to describe the merit obtained by the Bodhisattva when he first resolves his mind on becoming Enlightened. ISBN 0-917512-83-9, 200 pgs., $7.00

The Ten Inexhaustible Treasuries, Chapter 22. Explains the Ten Inexhaustible Treasuries attained by the Bodhisattva, which immediately proceed the Ten Conducts. ISBN 0-917512-38-3, 184 pgs., $7.00

Praises in the Tushita Heaven Palace, Chapter 24. Verses in praise of the Buddha spoken by the great Bodhisattvas after the Buddha had arrived in the Tushita Heaven, prior to Vajra Banner Bodhisattva's explanation of the Ten Transferences. ISBN 0-917512-39-1, 130 pgs., $5.00

Ten Transferences, Chapter 25, Part 1. Detailed prose and verse discussion of these important Bodhisattva stages. Contains the First Transference of Saving and Protecting Living Beings Apart From the Mark of Living Beings, and the Second Transference of Indestructibility which discusses faith. ISBN 0-917512-52-9, 250 pgs., $8.50

Ten Grounds, Chapter 26, Part 1. Contains the First Ground of Happiness, which focuses on the practice of giving. ISBN 0-917512-87-1, 234 pgs., $7.00. Part 2. Covers the Bodhisattva's Second Ground of Leaving Filth, Third Ground of Emitting Light, and the Fourth Ground of Blazing Wisdom. ISBN 0-917512-74-X, 200 pgs., $8.00

Further Volumes Forthcoming

十地品 *The Ten Grounds with commentary, in Zhung Wen. Three volume set $17.00*

Universal Worthy's Conduct, Chapter 36. *Universal Worthy Bodhisattva explains obstructions that arise from anger, gives methods to correct it, and describes the purities, wisdoms, universal entrances and supremely wonderous minds that result. ISBN 0-88139-011-9, 78 pgs., $7.50*

Entering the Dharma Realm, Chapter 39. *This chapter, which makes up one quarter of the entire Sutra, contains the spiritual journey of the Youth Good Wealth in his search for Ultimate Awakening. In his quest he meets fifty-three 'Good Teachers,' each of whom represents a successive stage on the Bodhisattva Path. The following volumes have been published to date:*

Part One. Describes the setting for the youth's quest, and his meeting with Manjushri Bodhisattva. ISBN 0-917512-68-5, 280 pgs., $8.50

Part Two. In this volume, Good Wealth meets his first ten teachers, who represent the positions of the Ten Dwellings. ISBN 0-917512-70-7, 250 pgs., $8.50

Part Three. In this volume, Good Wealth is taught by the ten teachers who correspond to the Ten Conducts. ISBN 0-917512-73-1, 250 pgs., $8.50

Part Four. In this volume, Good Wealth meets the ten teachers who represent the Bodhisattvas of the Ten Transferences. ISBN 0-917512-76-6, 185 pgs., $8.00

Part Five. In this volume, Good Wealth meets the six teachers who represent the first six Grounds. ISBN 0-917512-81-2, 300 pgs., $9.00

Part Six. Good Wealth meets the teachers on the seventh to tenth Grounds. ISBN 0-917512-48-0, 320 pgs., $9.00

Universal Worthy's Conduct and Vows, Chapter 40. *A detailed explanation of Universal Worthy Bodhisattva's ten great kinds of practice, considered to be the foremost of all practices. ISBN 0-917512-84-7, 300 pgs., $10.00 (In Zhung Wen, $4.00)*

華嚴經 *- World Rulers' Adornments, Chapter 1 to the Ten Transferences (parts 1 to 3), Chapter 25. In Zhung Wen only. Includes commentary. Ten Volume set $60.00. Vol. 9 $8.00; Vol. 10 $8.00.*

Heart Sutra and Verses Without a Stand - *Considered the most popular Sutra in the world today, the text of the HEART SUTRA explains the meaning of Prajna-paramita: the perfection of wisdom, which is able to clearly perceive the emptiness of all phenomena. Each line in the text is accompanied by an eloquent verse by the Venerable Master Hua, and his commentary contains an explanation of most of the fundamental Buddhist concepts. ISBN 0-917512-28-7, 160 pgs., $7.50*

心經非台頌解 *Same as HEART SUTRA above, including the commentary. In Zhung Wen. 120 pgs., $5.00*

Shurangama Sutra - *This Sutra gives the most detailed explanation of the Buddha's teachings concerning the mind. It includes an analysis of where the mind is located, an explanation of the origin of the cosmos, the specific workings of karma, a description of all the realms of existence, and the fifty kinds of deviant samadhi-concentrations which can delude us in our search for awakening. Also, in this Sutra, twenty-five enlightened Sages explain the methods they used to become enlightened. The entire eight volume set is available at a discounted price of $65.00.*

Volume One, *The Venerable Ananda presents seven ideas on the location of the mind, and the Buddha shows how each one is incorrect, and then explains the roots of the false and the true.* ISBN 0-917512-17-0, 289 pgs., $8.50

Volume Two, *The Buddha explains individual and collective karma, and reveals the true mind by displaying ten different aspects of the seeing-nature.* ISBN 0-917512-25-1, 212 pgs, $8.50

Volume Three, *The Buddha gives a clear description of the qualities of all the sensefields, their respective consciousnesses, and all the internal and external elemental forces of the universe. He explains how all are ultimately unreal, neither existing through causes nor arising spontaneously.* ISBN 0-917512-94-4, 240 pgs, $8.50

Volume Four, *The Buddha talks about the formation of the world, the coming into being of sentient creatures, and the cycle of karmic retribution.* ISBN 0-917512-90-1, 200 pgs, $8.50

Volume Five, *Twenty-five Sages explain the method they used to transcend the realm of birth and death. Manjushri Bodhisattva selects the method used by the Bodhisattva Kuan Yin of 'returning the hearing to listen to the self-nature,' as the most appropriate for people in our world-system.* ISBN 0-917512-91-X, 250 pgs., $8.50

Volume Six, *Includes the Buddha's explanation of the Four Clear and Unalterable Instructions on Purity, how to establish a Bodhimandala, the Shurangama Mantra and its wondrous functions, and the 12 categories of living beings.* ISBN 0-917512-97-9, 200 pgs., $8.50

Volume Seven, *Contains an explanation of the 55 stages of the Bodhisattva's path to Enlightenment, how beings fall into the hells, all the realms of existence of the ghosts, animals, people, immortals, and the various heavens.* ISBN 0-917512-97-9, 270 pgs., $8.50

Volume Eight, *In this, the final volume, the Buddha explains the Fifty Skandha Demon States, which cultivators may get stuck in.* ISBN 0-917512-35-9, $8.50 (Available August, 1983)

楞嚴經淺釋 Zhung Wen. Volume I, $5.00

Sixth Patriarch Sutra - *One of the foremost scriptures of Ch'an (Zen) Buddhism, this text describes the life and teachings of the remarkable Patriarch of the T'ang Dynasty, Great Master Hui Neng, who, though unable to read or write, was enlightened to the true nature of all things.* ISBN 0-917512-19-7, 235 pgs., $10.00 (Hardcover: $15.00)

Sutra in 42 Sections - *In this Sutra, which was the first to be transported from India and translated into Zhung Wen, the Buddha gives the most essential instructions for cultivating the Dharma, emphasizing the cardinal virtues of renunciation, contentment, and patience.* ISBN 0-917512-15-4, 114 pgs., $4.00

Sutra of the Past Vows of Earth Store Bodhisattva - *This Sutra tells how Earth Store Bodhisattva attained his position as one of the greatest Bodhisattvas, foremost in vows. It also explains the workings of karma, how beings undergo rebirth, and the various kinds of hells. This is the first English translation.* Hardcover only, ISBN 0-917512-09-X, 235 pgs., $16.00. *English text without commentary, for recitation, also available.* ISBN 0-88139-502-1, 120 pgs., $6.00.

地藏菩薩本願經淺釋　　*Same as the Earth Store Sutra above, including the commentary. In Zhung Wen,* 140 pgs., $6.50.

City of 10,000 Buddhas Recitation Handbook　萬佛城日誦儀規 *Has all the material covered in the traditional daily morning, afternoon, and evening services and special services recited in Buddhist monasteries in the East and West. Includes scriptures, praises, chants, mantras, repentances, and so forth. Bi-lingual edition, Zhung Wen/English* 240 pgs., $6.00 (2nd edition).

Vajra Prajna Paramita (Diamond) Sutra - *One of the most popular scriptures, the VAJRA SUTRA explains how the Bodhisattva relies on the perfection of wisdom to teach and transform beings.* ISBN 0-917512-02-2, 192 pgs., $8.00.

COMMENTARIAL LITERATURE:

Buddha Root Farm - *A collection of lectures given during an Amitabha recitation session which explains the practice and philosophy of the Pure Land School. The instructions are very complete, and are especially useful for a beginner.* ISBN 0-917512-08-1, 72 pgs. $4.00.

Great Compassion Dharma Transmission Verses of the Forty-two Hands and Eyes - *Contains 42 b/w photographs of the Venerable Master Hua's self-portrait paintings of the 42 Hands and Eyes, and 42 b/w photographs of copper reliefs of the mudras, with verses by the Venerable Master (with English translation) for each one.* ISBN 0-88139-002-X, 100 pgs., $16.00.

Herein Lies the Treasure-trove, *Volume I. Various talks given by the Venerable Master at the City of 10,000 Buddhas during recent years.* ISBN 0-88139-001-1, 250 pgs., $8.50.

Filiality: The Source of Virtue - *Filiality is the very root of Way-virtue. It is the single most vital force that sustains the universe. Therefore, it is only natural that Buddhist disciples base their conduct on an attitude of filial piety and respect, for their parents and elders, for the rulers and officials of countries and the world, for the Triple Jewel, and ultimately, for all living beings, for all beings have at one time or another been our parents. Vols. I and II of this series contain stories from the 24 famous tales of filial paragons of Zhung Kuo (China), and numerous excerpts from Buddhist Sutras about filial behavior.* Vol. I, ISBN 0-88139-019-4, 120 pgs., $7.00; Vol. II, ISBN 0-88139-020-8, 120 pgs., $7.00

Life-pulse of Living Beings - *Instructions on not killing, the detrimental karmic effects and health hazards related to eating meat, and stories of reincarnation concerning these.* ISBN 0-88139-006-2, 250 pgs., $8.50

Listen to Yourself, Think Everything Over - *Vols. I and II - Instructions on how to practice the method of reciting the name of the Buddhas and Bodhisattvas, along with a straightforward explanation of how to cultivate Ch'an meditation. All instructions were given during actual meditation and recitation sessions.* ISBN 0-917512-24-3, 153 pgs., $7.00

Shramanera Vinaya and Rules of Deportment - *The Buddha instructed his disciples to take the Vinaya (the Monastic Moral Code) as their master once he himself had entered Nirvana. This text, by Great Master Lien Ch'ih of the Ming Dynasty, explains the moral code for novice Monks and Nuns.* ISBN 0-917512-04-9, 112 pgs., $4.00

沙彌律儀要略釋   *Same as Shramanera Vinaya, including the* commentary. *In Zhung Wen.* 105 pgs., $5.00

Shastra On The Door to Understanding The Hundred Dharmas - *A text fundamental to Consciousness Only doctrine, by Vasubandhu Bodhisattva, with commentary by the Venerable Master Hua.* ISBN 0-88139-003-8, 130 pgs., $6.50

Shurangama Mantra Commentary - 楞嚴咒疏句偈解
Verses and commentary by the Venerable Hua on this Ancient text explaining how to practice the foremost mantra in the Buddha's teaching, including a line-by-line analysis of the mantra. The first volume contains all the instructions on how to prepare before holding the mantra and an explanation of the first portion of the mantra. ISBN 0-917512-69-3, 296 pgs., $8.50 (Bi-lingual, Zhung Wen and English). *Vol. II contains an explanation of lines 30-90 of the mantra.* ISBN 0-917512-82-0, 200 pgs., $7.50, Vol. III, lines 91-145, ISBN 0-917512-36-7, 160 pgs., $6.50. *Vol. IV, Available Summer, 1983.*

楞嚴咒疏   *Text of the above, without the commentary of the Venerable Master Hua. In Zhung Wen,* $5.00

Song of Enlightenment - *The famous lyric poem of the state of the Ch'an Sage, by the Venerable Master Yung Chia of the T'ang Dynasty. (Available Summer, 1983)*

永嘉大師證道歌詮釋 *- same as above in Zhung Wen, with commentary.* 40 pgs., $2.50

The Ten Dharma Realms are not Beyond a Single Thought - *Eloquent poems composed by the Venerable Hua, on all the realms of being, which are accompanied by extensive commentarial material and drawings.* ISBN 0-917512-12-X, 72 pgs., $4.00

Water-Mirror Reflecting Heaven - *An essay on the fundamental principle of cause and effect, with biographical material on contemporary Buddhist cultivation in Zhung Kuo. Clear and to the point; very readable for young and old.* ISBN 0-88139-501-3, 82 pgs., $4.00

水鏡回天錄 - *Same as Water-Mirror above, with the commentary. In Zhung Wen.* 130 pgs., $5.00

宣化上人開示錄（一）- *Instructional talks in Zhung Wen.* 190 pgs., $5.00

宣化上人開示錄（二）- *Volume 2,* $6.50

宣化上人偈讚錄 - *Verses in Zhung Wen, including verses for each of the 84 lines of the Great Compassion Mantra.* 150 pgs., $5.

萬佛城聯語集 - *Matched couplets by cultivators at the City of 10,000 Buddhas. In Zhung Wen.,* 82 pgs., $4.00

BIOGRAPHICAL:

Pictorial Biography of the Venerable Master Hsü Yün - *Prose and verses written by the Venerable Hua illustrated with brush drawings, documenting Venerable Yün's life. Will be a two-volume set. Volume 1 contains 104 sections of prose, verses, and drawings. Volume 2 contains 208.* ISBN 0-88139-008-9, 120 pgs., $7.00

Records of High Sanghans - *A living tradition is sustained to the extent that it is embodied in its heroes. The Buddhist tradition is enhanced by a large body of literature containing truly moving and inspiring life-stories of monks and nuns who dedicated their bodies and lives to the preservation and propagation of the Sagely Teachings. Vol. 1 will cover the life-stories of the first eminent Sanghans who brought the Buddhadharma from India to Zhung Kuo, and the adventures of those first Sanghans who withstood severe trials and hardships as they translated the first Sutras from Indian languages into Zhung Wen (Chinese).* ISBN 0-88139-012-7, 158 pgs., $7.00

Records of the Life of the Venerable Master Hsüan Hua - *The life and teachings of the Venerable Master from his birthplace in Zhung Kuo to the present time in America:*

Volume One, covers the Ven. Master's life in Zhung Kuo. ISBN 0-917512-07-3, 96 pgs., $5.00 (Also available in Spanish, $8.00).
Volume Two, covers the events of the Master's life as he cultivated and taught in Hong Kong, containing many photos, poems, and stories. ISBN 0-917512-10-3, 220 pgs., $8.00

Further Volumes Forthcoming

宣化禪師事蹟 - *A separate biographical work in Zhung Wen covering the Venerable Master's life in Zhung Kuo and Hong Kong.* 84 pgs., $4.00

Three Steps, One Bow - *The daily journal of American Bhikshus Heng Ju and Heng Yo, who, in 1973-74, made a pilgrimage for world peace from Gold Mountain Monastery in San Francisco to Seattle, Washington, making a full prostration every third step. The pilgrimage was inspired by monks in ancient Zhung Kuo, who would bow every third step for thousands of miles to a famous monastery or renowned teacher.* ISBN 0-917512-18-9, 160 pgs., $5.00

World Peace Gathering - *A collection of instructional talks on Buddhism commemorating the successful completion of the bowing pilgrimage of Bhikshus Heng Ju and Heng Yo.* ISBN 0-917512-05-7, 128 pgs., $5.00

News From True Cultivators - *The letters written by the two "Three Steps, One Bow" monks (Dharma Master's Sure & Ch'au), during their bowing pilgrimage, addressed to the Venerable Abbot and the Assembly of the City of Ten Thousand Buddhas, are uplifting messages to those traversing the Path of cultivation and inspiring exhortations to all those concerned with evolving vital and workable methods to alleviate the acute problems of our troubled times. The language is simple, the insights are profound. No one should miss reading this book.* ISBN 0-88139-016-X

With One Heart Bowing to the City of 10,000 Buddhas - *The moving journals of American Bhikshus Heng Sure and Heng Ch'au, who made a "three steps, one bow" pilgrimage from Gold Wheel Temple in Los Angeles to the City of 10,000 Buddhas, located 110 miles north of San Francisco, from May, 1977, to October, 1979.*

> Volume One, *May 6 - June 30, 1977.* ISBN 0-917512-21-9. 180 pgs., $6
> Volume Two, *July 1 - October 30, 1977.* ISBN 0-917512-23-5, 322 pgs., $7.00
> Volume Three, *October 30 - December 20, 1977.* ISBN 0-917512-89-8, 154 pgs., $5.00
> Volume Four, *December 17 - January 21, 1978.* ISBN 0-917512-90-1, 136 pgs., $4.00
> Volume Five, *January 28 - February 18, 1978.* ISBN 0-917512-91-X, 127 pgs., $4.00
> Volume Six, *February 19 - April 2, 1978.* ISBN 0-917512-92-8, 200 pgs., $6.00
> Volume Seven, *April 3 - May 24, 1978.* ISBN 0-917512-99-5, 160 pgs., $5.00
> Volume Eight, *May 24 - September, 1978.* ISBN 0-917512-53-7. 232 pgs., $7.50
> Volume Nine, *September - October, 1978.* ISBN 0-88139-016-X, 232 pgs., $7.50

Further Volumes Forthcoming

修行者的消息 *-The complete collection of letters written by Bhikshus Heng Sure and Heng Ch'au during their 2½ year bowing pilgrimage to the City of 10,000 Buddhas; In Zhung Wen. Two-volume set,* $10.00

精進者的日記 (一) *- Part One of the Journals of the Bowing Monks; in Zhung Wen,* $6.00

精進者的日記 (二) *-Part Two of the Journals of the Bowing Monks; in Zhung Wen,* $6.50

Open Your Eyes; Take a Look at the World - *The Journals of Bhikshus Heng Sure and Heng Ch'au, and Bhikshuni Heng Tao, written during the 1978 Asia-region visit by the Venerable Master and other members of the Sino-American Buddhist Association.* ISBN 0-917512-32-4. *347 pgs., $7.50.*

放眼觀世界 *- Same as Open Your Eyes...; in Zhung Wen,*
347 pgs., $7.50.

Heng Ch'au's Journal - *An account of the remarkable experiences and changes undergone by Bhikshu Heng Ch'au when he first came in contact with Gold Mountain Monastery. 112 pgs., $1.95.*

CHILDREN'S BOOKS

Cherishing Life - *Contains verses and brush drawings about not taking life, and public records about cause and effect drawn from actual events recorded by Dharma Masters, giving people's memories of past lives as animals, and their awareness of the reasons for their retributions of being in the animal realm. For elementary-age children, as well as adults. ISBN 0-88139-004-6, 150 pgs., $7.*

Human Roots: Buddhist Stories for Young Readers - *Has a total of 14 stories from the Buddhist Canon and historical records. ISBN 0-88139-500-S, 95 pgs., $4.00.*

MUSIC, NOVELS, AND BROCHURES

Songs for Awakening - *Words and music of over forty modern American Buddhist songs, indexed according to title and first line, with drawings, woodcuts, and photographs. The picturesque, 9" X 12" Songbook makes a fine gift to introduce your friends to Buddhism. ISBN 0-917512-31-7, 112 pgs., $7.95.*

Awakening - *Recorded on cassette tape, ten Buddhist songs set in Western style (all in English), ranging from pop to rock, to folk and country. Subjects covered include: Bodhisattva vows, the I Ching, Ch'an meditation, Lao-Tzu, the Lotus Sutra, an Abhidharma meditation, Amita Buddha and his Pure Land. $7.00 plus $1.00 shipping in the U.S.A. and $2.00 for international orders.*

The Three Cart Patriarch - *A 12" stereo lp., recorded by and for children, based on the "Monkey" tales of Zhung Kuo which features stories, six musical productions, and many special effects. $7.00 plus $1.00 shipping in the U.S.A. and $2.00 for international orders*

City of 10,000 Buddhas Color Brochure - *Over 30 color photos of the scenic center for world Buddhism, along with many poems and a description of its activities. 24 pgs., $2.00.*

Dharma Realm Buddhist University Catalog, 1983 - *ISBN 0-88139-000-3, 246 pages., $5.00. (Available Summer, 1983)*

Celebrisi's Journey - *A novel by David Rounds, describing the events in a modern American's quest for enlightenment. (First edition) ISBN 0-917512-14-6, 178 pgs., $4.00.*

吳佛城室釰善提海

VAJRA BODHI SEA

Vajra Bodhi Sea *is a monthly journal of orthodox Buddhism, which* has been published by the Sino-American Buddhist Association since 1970. Each issue contains the most recent translation work of the Buddhist Text Translation Society. Each issue includes a biography of a great Patriarch of Buddhism from the ancient past, sketches of the lives of contemporary monastics and lay-followers around the world, a Sanskrit lesson, articles on practice, and other material. The journal is bi-lingual, in Zhung Wen and English with 24 pages each, in an 8½" by 11" format. Single issues $2.50; one year subscription $26.00; and three years subscription $70.00. ISBN 0-507-6986 (postage is included in the subscription fee).

POSTAGE AND HANDLING

United States - $1.25 for the first book and $.40 for each additional book. All publications are sent via special fourth-class. Allow from 4 days to 2 weeks for delivery.

International - $1.50 for the first book and $.75 for each additional book. All publications are sent via "book rate" or direct mail sack (surface). For countries, such as Indonesia and Malaysia, in which parcels may be lost, we suggest orders be sent via registered mail for an additional $3.25 per parcel of 10 books each. We cannot be responsible for parcels lost in the mail. Allow 6 to 8 weeks for delivery.

The rates noted above for postage and handling are given as an indication of actual costs. On large orders, purchasers may wish to submit their order for a more precise estimate of postage and handling costs.

All orders require pre-payment before they will be processed.

中文佛書目錄

大方廣佛華嚴經十地品淺釋（平裝三冊）　美國萬佛城宣化上人講解。

第一冊（第一歡喜地）（漢英對照）　定價美金七元。

第二冊（第二離垢地。第三發光地。第四燄慧地。第五難勝地）　定價美金五元。

第三冊（第六現前地。第七遠行地。第八不動地。第九善慧地。第十法雲地）定價美金六元。

千手千眼大悲心陀羅尼經（全一冊）　定價美金六元。

般若波羅蜜多心經非台頌解（全一冊）　美國萬佛城宣化上人講解　定價美金五元。

楞嚴咒疏句偈解（漢英對照）（第一冊）　美國萬佛城宣化上人講解　定價美金八元五角。

梵網經講錄（漢英對照）（上冊）　慧僧法師述　定價美金十元。

梵網經講錄（漢英對照）（下冊）　定價美金八元。

地藏菩薩本願經淺釋　定價美金六元五角

佛書部分：

永嘉大師證道歌詮釋（全一冊）　美國萬佛城宣化上人講解　定價美金二元五角。

緇門崇行錄　蓮池大師著　弘一大師集（贈閱）

宣化上人偈讚聞釋錄（全一冊）　定價美金五元

宣化禪師事蹟（全一冊）　定價美金四元。

放眼觀世界（亞洲弘法記）、全一冊）　定價美金七元五角

修行者的消息（二步一拜兩行者一心頂禮萬佛城之來鴻）　定價美金七元

佛教精進者的日記（平裝上冊）　定價美金六元。

總流通處：

中美佛教總會萬佛城
The Sino-American Buddhist
    Association, INC.
Headquarters: City of Ten
    Thousand Buddhas
P.O.BOX 217, Talmage,
Talmage, CA 95481, USA
Tel: (707) 462-0939

三藩市分會金山禪寺
San Francisco Branch: Gold
    Mountain Monastery
1731 15th Street
San Francisco, CA 94103
Tel: (415) 626-4204, 861-9672

三藩市國際譯經學院
The International Institute for
    the Translation of Buddhist Texts
3636 Washington Street
San Francisco, CA 94118-
Tel: (415) 921-9570

洛杉磯分會金輪寺
Los Angeles Branch: Gold Wheel
    Temple
1728 W. 6th Street
Los Angeles, CA 90017
Tel: (213) 483-7497

萬佛城聯語集（一） 定價美金四元

水鏡回天錄（全一冊）美國萬佛城宣化上人著 定價美金五元

沙彌律儀要略解（全一冊）美國萬佛城宣化上人講解 定價美金五元

楞嚴咒疏句偈解（漢英對照）（第二冊） 定價美金七元五角

宣化上人語錄 定價美金五元

即將出版：

大方廣佛華嚴經淺釋（十定品至入法界品）

大佛頂首楞嚴經淺釋

佛教精進者的日記（下冊）

中美佛教總會法界大學出版

Dharma Protector Wei T'o Bodhisattva

Verse of Transference

May the merit and virtue accrued from this work,
Adorn the Buddhas' Pure Lands,
Repaying four kinds of kindness above,
And aiding those suffering in the paths below.

May those who see and hear of this,
All bring forth the resolve for Bodhi,
And when this retribution body is over,
Be born together in ultimate bliss.